Agnès Varda |

Contemporary Film Directors

Edited by Justus Nieland and Jennifer Fay

The Contemporary Film Directors series provides concise, well-written introductions to directors from around the world and from every level of the film industry. Its chief aims are to broaden our awareness of important artists, to give serious critical attention to their work, and to illustrate the variety and vitality of contemporary cinema. Contributors to the series include an array of internationally respected critics and academics. Each volume contains an incisive critical commentary, an informative interview with the director, and a detailed filmography.

A list of books in the series
appears at the end of this book.

Agnès Varda

Kelley Conway

**UNIVERSITY
OF
ILLINOIS
PRESS**
URBANA,
CHICAGO,
AND
SPRINGFIELD

Frontispiece: Agnès Varda (Julia Fabry, 2012). © Ciné-Tamaris

Library of Congress Control Number: 2015950937
ISBN 978-0-252-03972-0 (hardcover)
ISBN 978-0-252-08120-0 (paperback)
ISBN 978-0-252-09782-9 (e-book)

Permission has been granted to reprint portions of the following essays:
Conway, Kelley. "A New Wave of Spectators: Contemporary Responses to *Cleo from 5 to 7, Film Quarterly* 61, no. 1 (Fall 2007): 38–47.
Conway, Kelley. "The New Wave in the Museum: Varda, Godard, and the Multi-Media Installation." *Contemporary French Civilization* 32, no. 2 (Summer 2008): 195–217.

Contents |

Acknowledgments |

When I first met Agnès Varda during a 2002 retrospective and conference I had organized at the University of Wisconsin–Madison, I did not yet have plans to write a book about her work. Instead I was immersed in the completion of another book and in caring for my two-month-old baby, Charlotte. Varda's enthusiastic engagement at that conference, however, laid the groundwork for a warm personal connection and an emphatic invitation to visit her production complex the next time I was in Paris. A few years later, on my first trip to Ciné-Tamaris, Varda's Paris base on the rue Daguerre, my plans changed abruptly. The richness of the Ciné-Tamaris archive, Varda's personal generosity, and her expansion into installation art convinced me to embark on what became the most compelling project of my professional life so far.

Thanks, above all, to Agnès Varda for opening her archive to me and for her engagement with this project. Thanks to Rosalie Demy-Varda and Mathieu Demy for their tireless work in the preservation and restoration of the films of their parents, Agnès Varda and Jacques Demy. I am beyond grateful for the patience and help of the amazing team at Ciné-Tamaris: Anita Benoliel, Julia Fabry, Fanny Lautissier, Jean-Baptiste Morin, Cecilia Rose, and Stéphanie Scanvic. Film historian Bernard Bastide, former member of the *belle équipe* at Ciné-Tamaris, has been particularly generous with his insights about Varda's filmmaking process. Thank you Cecilia Rose for supplying illustrations for the book at the very last moment in the wake of a computer crisis. Special thanks are also due to my research assistant, Laura Gross, fellow Iowan, former Ciné-Tamaris intern, UW-Madison graduate, and my indefatigable partner on this journey from Madison to Paris to Noirmoutier and back. Thanks also to the ever-professional and patient team at the University of Illinois Press, Jennifer Fay, Justus Nieland, Daniel Nasset, and Marika Christofides.

Delivering portions of this research at conferences was enormously helpful in the sharpening of my arguments. Thank you Eric Thouvenal and Roxanne Hamery for organizing an amazing conference in 2007 devoted to the work of Varda at the Université de Rennes. I am also grateful to the Screenwriting Research Network, which allowed me to share my research with its members in Brussels in 2012 and in Madison in 2013. Nathalie Rachlin and Rosemarie Scullion organized perhaps the most intense and pleasurable conference I have ever attended, the "Contemporary French Cinema and the Crisis of Globalization," sponsored by the Borchard Foundation and held at the Chateau de la Bretesche in 2012.

Many scholars and friends share my belief in the importance of Varda's work and have inspired and helped me at various stages of this project. David Gardner, one of the best writers I know, generously took time away from his busy career in television to help me polish my prose and to translate the interview with Varda. Fellow scholars of French cinema Janet Bergstrom, Betsy Bogart McCabe, Colin Burnett, Maggie Flinn, Sandy Flitterman-Lewis, Claudia Gorbman, Charlie Michael, Richard Neupert, Geneviève Van Cauwenberg, and Alan Williams have taught me much. The members of my 2013 Varda seminar at the UW-Madison inspired me enormously, as do my wonderful colleagues Maria Belodubrovskaya, David Bordwell, Eric Hoyt, Lea Jacobs, Vance Kepley, J. J. Murphy, Ben Singer, Jeff Smith, and Kristin Thompson. Michael Trevis was exceptionally helpful in helping me choose illustrations for the book. I am fortunate to have good friends in Paris and Madison, such as David Gardner, Gillian Ludwig, Angela Giovinazzo, Nelly Boireau, Susan Zaeske, Mary Louise Roberts, and Jerilyn Goodman, who share my appreciation of Varda.

Archival research requires considerable resources. I am deeply grateful for the Hamel Family Faculty Research Grants, a UW-Madison Graduate Summer Research Grant, and grants from the UW-Madison Anonymous Fund and the Wisconsin Humanities Council in support of "Landscape and Portrait: Agnès Varda's Cinematic Geographies," a film retrospective and international conference held at UW-Madison in 2002.

Without the unwavering encouragement and love of Patrick, Sullivan, and Charlotte Sweet, this book would not exist. I dedicate this book to my family.

Agnès Varda |

New Wave Cinéaste to Digital Gleaner

Change and Continuity in the Work of Agnès Varda

It is hardly news that Agnès Varda is fond of (one might venture besotted by) Paris's 14th arrondissement, where she has made her home since first arriving on the rue Daguerre in 1951. She devoted an entire film to the daily lives and preoccupations of the denizens of her beloved rue Daguerre, *Daguerréotypes* (1974). Her second feature film, *Cléo de 5 à 7* (*Cleo from 5 to 7*, 1962) is largely set in that southern arrondissement, cradled between the green swaths of the Luxembourg Gardens to the north and the Parc Montsouris to the south. To the west beckons Montparnasse and its nightlife, while the vast walled prison and hospital complexes bordering the neighboring 13th discourage further exploration eastward. Cleo's trajectory in the film constitutes a classic Left Bank idyll that places Paris's 14th at the epicenter of the known world. She begins her journey in the home of a fortune teller on rue du Rivoli in the 1st arrondissement and moves south, across the Seine, to her apartment in Montparnasse. She skirts the Latin Quarter and the Sorbonne, where student restlessness is already evident on the margins of the bland postwar prosperity as the Algerian conflict played out. She then strolls through the 14th arrondissement for much of the remainder of the film, moving from a café in Montparnasse to the nearby train station and eventually to that very Parc Montsouris on the southern edge of the city, where she meets a soldier on leave from Algeria. Her trajectory ends portentously in the 13th, at the Salpêtrière Hospital, once a repository for prostitutes, the poor, and the criminally insane, where a diagnosis of cancer is confirmed.

In some sense, *Cleo* perfectly demonstrates Varda's prescience: her film anticipates student unrest, reflects on upheaval and conflict in the Maghreb, and more broadly, if literally for Cleo, foretells the societal ills to come. Varda sees these written in the city itself, its landmarks, iconic quarters, and stone façades. And she shows Cleo seeing these things, seeing with a woman's gaze, a decade before Laura Mulvey would attempt to formulate looking outside of male subjectivity. Clearly this is one reason feminist theorists and critics have taken up Varda's work so readily.

Varda's own trajectory, through her career and in the world, will guide my work here. Born in Ixelles, Belgium, in 1928 to a Greek father and a French mother, Varda spent her adolescence in Sète, a fishing village in the south of France. At seventeen, she moved to Paris to finish her high school education and to attend classes at the Sorbonne and the Ecole du Louvre. With the exception of two lengthy sojourns to Los Angeles, she has lived at the same address on the rue Daguerre in Paris since the early 1950s.

Like Cleo, it's hard not to picture Varda in the 14th arrondissement, where she is both at home and at work. Varda is all too aware of the distinction between local and tourist, between villager and visitor, and it is a contrast that gives texture to much of her work. Window shoppers on the rue Daguerre should not be surprised to find Varda herself peddling DVD collections of Jacques Demy's and her own work in her shopfront studio Ciné-Tamaris, or unloading groceries or suitcases from the trunk of her car at the sprawling residence across the street. Deep in research in Ciné-Tamaris's archives, I myself have been pleasantly interrupted by Varda coming and going, insisting I break from my work to join her for lunch. Her door seems always to be open, and the world knows where to find her; imagine my shock answering the doorbell while

Varda is rummaging through binders of old reviews or interviews on my behalf, only to discover Jean-Pierre Léaud or Anouk Aimée, in the neighborhood and hoping to find Varda at home. But if she is unpacking suitcases, it is because she has returned from an extended stay at her beloved Ile de Noirmoutier, spitting distance from Nantes, where her filmmaker husband Jacques Demy grew up. And despite the heavy gravitational pull of the 14th arrondissement, Varda's career has taken her from Languedoc to the gritty streets of Oakland, from Hollywood to Havana. Each of the sections in this study traces stages of Varda's journey, each place shaping her art and her vision of the world, shifting her identification between visitor and local.

Agnès Varda's rise to the top tier of international, independent filmmakers can be framed in a paradox. In 1954, a twenty-five-year-old woman with neither training in film production nor connections in the film industry began work on a film called *La Pointe Courte* (1955), which both evoked Italian Neorealism and anticipated by a full five years the French New Wave. The film, made completely outside the hierarchical system of French film production of the 1950s, provides a realist chronicle of daily life in a fishing village and a stylized treatment of the troubled marriage of a bourgeois Parisian couple. Varda financed the film by forming a cooperative made up of the film's cast and crew (a young Alain Resnais, a year away from releasing *Nuit et brouillard* [*Night and Fog*, 1955], generously agreed to join the cooperative and edit her film). Not until the late 1950s would French directors conduct similarly unconventional experiments in narrative structure, style, and mode of production. *La Pointe Courte* was denied a traditional theatrical release but was nevertheless reviewed favorably by André Bazin, who called the film "miraculous" and praised its combination of documentary simplicity and modernist stylization. How did *La Pointe Courte* happen and where did Varda go from there? Moving from this work to those that follow, how can we best explain and appreciate Varda's melding of documentary authenticity, stylistic experimentation, and social commentary? How have her working methods changed through time? These questions are central to this study.

Varda's trajectory through film history conforms neither to the traditional story film historians tend to tell about the French New Wave, as Richard Neupert adeptly makes clear in his 2007 history of the movement, nor to our sense of the conventional trajectory of independent filmmakers more generally. Varda was a professional photographer whose initial aesthetic commitments were framed by Modernist literature and Renaissance painting as much as anything else. Although historically placed in the category of the "Left Bank" with the likes of Resnais and Chris Marker, Varda's directorial persona and her films differ significantly from those of the Left Bank directors and should be understood on their own terms. Moreover, Varda's career, spanning more than half a century and still going strong, has been unusually varied. Rather than making only fiction features, Varda has alternated between creating documentaries and fiction films, short and feature-length films, photography, and installation art. This unusual heterogeneity and exuberance in Varda's work deserves further exploration, as do both the consistency and the changes in Varda's aesthetic preoccupations and working methods over the years.

Despite Agnès Varda's centrality to the New Wave, to European art cinema, to experimental documentary, and to feminist film history, her work has received far less critical attention than it deserves. Varda's written autobiography, *Varda par Agnès*, remains a precious resource on her life and work to 1994, but this volume unfortunately has never been translated into English and is now out of print. Until recently, the only monograph on Varda in English was Alison Smith's valuable *Agnès Varda*, but that study concludes with the late 1990s. Since then, Varda has embarked on a new phase in her career: in 2000, she made *Les Glaneurs et la glaneuse* (*The Gleaners and I*), her first digital film, and in 2003 she exhibited her first multimedia installation at the Venice Biennale, *Patatutopia*. In 2006, she exhibited a suite of installations, *L'île et elle* (*The Island and She*), at the Fondation Cartier in Paris, and in 2008 Varda followed up with a feature-length documentary, *Les Plages d'Agnès* (*The Beaches of Agnès*), which retooled the aesthetics evident in her installations toward a cinematic memoir. These works initiated a new chapter in Varda's long and productive career, one that remains ongoing and thereby calls for continued investigation.

If, as I've suggested, Varda was unfairly neglected by film critics and historians in the past, happily the same cannot be said today. In addition to the scores of articles and book chapters devoted to her films and installations, several book-length studies of Varda's work are now available and more are under way. Varda's greatest commercial success, *Sans toit ni loi* (*Vagabond*, 1985) drew a generation of feminist critics to re-examine thirty years of filmmaking. Thus did Sandy Flitterman-Lewis provide what I believe is a definitive and still current feminist account of Varda's work, *To Desire Differently*, despite its publication nearly twenty years ago. Flitterman-Lewis focuses on the representation of femininity in *La Pointe Courte*, *Cleo*, and *Vagabond*, deftly combining a sophisticated analysis of Varda's feminist aesthetics (through an emphasis on the key issues of feminist film theory, including vision, subjectivity, and desire) with an analysis of the broader context of French feminist filmmaking that takes into account the work of Germaine Dulac and Marie Epstein. Smith's 1998 monograph explores, among other topics, the "specifically feminine" aspects of five films (*L'Opéra-Mouffe / Diary of a Pregnant Woman*, 1958; *Cleo*; *Réponse de femmes: Notre corps, notre sexe / Women Reply*, 1975; *L'Une chante, l'autre pas / One Sings, the Other Doesn't*, 1977; and *Vagabond*), framing her analysis with the question, "How to represent the feminine?" (93). Rebecca DeRoo's two published essays fruitfully position *Le Bonheur* (*Happiness*, 1965) and *One Sings* in fresh contexts: the representation of femininity in 1960s women's magazines and Brechtian performance, respectively. With this rich terrain so fruitfully mined already, I will not be focusing on Varda's role as a feminist filmmaker so much as her work as a woman making films in France.

Beyond the framework of feminism, Neupert's *A History of the French New Wave* positions Varda in the context of that movement. Delphine Bénézet focuses on Varda's lesser-known films (including *Opéra-Mouffe*, *Daguerréotypes*, and *Mur Murs / Mural Murals*, 1981), interpreting Varda's concerns through the lens of phenomenology and ethics. A collection of Varda's interviews was recently edited and translated by T. Jefferson Kline and will no doubt enhance Varda's reputation as one of the most insightful analysts of her own work. Again, with so much substantial scholarship on the historical (and political) context of the New Wave and Varda's project through the tumultuous 1960s and 1970s, I will not try to expand on that line of inquiry here. I will, however, engage with underutilized sources in French about Varda's work, including her autobiography, *Varda par Agnès*, and the collected papers from the first conference ever devoted to Varda's work in France, *Agnès*

Varda Le cinéma et au-delà, edited by Antony Fiant, Roxane Hamery, and Eric Thouvenel (Presses Universitaires de Rennes, 2007). I was also fortunate enough to have access to Bernard Bastide's invaluable, unpublished dissertation detailing the conception, production, and reception of *Cleo*.

For a critical reading of *Cleo*, both Valerie Orpen and Steven Ungar have contributed valuable book-length analyses. The film has in fact already elicited so many rich analyses of space, time, and characterization, in these studies and those of Flitterman-Lewis and Susan Hayward, that I have not included here an extended reading of my own, focusing instead on reconstructing the postwar cinephilic culture of France and *Cleo*'s place within it. My take on the *ciné-club*'s role in revitalizing postwar French culture and detailed analysis of survey responses to *Cleo* solicited by Varda herself (and currently held in the Ciné-Tamaris archive) offers a new perspective about the film's circulation through France of the early 1960s, one far less familiar to historians of French cinema.

Indeed, my approach to *Cleo* and to all the films and installations I explore in this book begins with the assumption that authorship in the production of moving images is still eminently worthy of study. In the wake of the poststructuralist turn, one can well understand how it became unfashionable to place the living, breathing film director at the center of one's research. And yet most film historians never really lost interest in discovering the aesthetic and narrative preoccupations of individual filmmakers. My particular contribution to the scholarly literature on Varda is borne in large part of my lucky access to her archive over a period of many years and to my sense that attempting to chart the changes and the continuity in her working methods would yield interesting information about her work and one artist's approach to the creative process. Writing film history from the point of view of authorship means charting the thematic and stylistic consistencies of a filmmaker's work over time, but it also, for me, increasingly means writing the most detailed history of film production possible. Discovering the concrete details of the emergence of a given project, the development and shifting forms of its screenplay, the search for financing, the casting, the shoot, the editing, the exhibition, and reception are essential to the questions that interest me most about Varda. (How and why does she make her films and installations? How can we chart their impact in the culture, both commercially and critically?) Therefore these questions, so central to Varda's journey through the cinematic and art scene landscape, will benefit from the greatest share of my attention. My vision of film authorship holds that while directors are certainly acted upon by forces outside of themselves, they also seek challenges and solve problems, maintain certain aesthetic commitments (but abandon others over time), and impose creative constraints on themselves (while resisting others).

I recall having breakfast with Varda in Montreal in October of 2005. She had come to town to speak at the retrospective on her work at the Cinémathèque québécoise and to hang an accompanying exhibition of her photographs. We were seated by the window of a hotel dining room, several floors above street level. As we chatted, Varda looked out the window and spotted some homeless people across the street. Some stood, others sat; some moved about a bit, many were encumbered with bags. Varda could not take her eyes off of them and wondered aloud, "What do you think they're carrying in those bags? Where do you think they sleep at night?" She observed their movements carefully for many minutes. Much later, in June 2012, I saw an exhibition of Varda installations in Nantes. One of them, *La Chambre occupée (The Occupied Room)*, consisted of a decrepit room hidden away above the elegant covered shopping arcade, the Passage Pommeraye, made famous in Jacques Demy's *Lola* (1961). Made to look like a squat, the room housed an assemblage comprising a mattress propped upright, a shopping cart holding a microwave oven, and an old stove. Video monitors installed in the mattress, the microwave, and the stove screened footage of homeless people, moving about and speaking of their plight. Thinking back to her intense observation of the homeless people in Montreal, I understood that Varda never stops looking and thinking and working. She looks at the world around her with a rare intensity and empathy and then transforms her thoughts and emotions into new work.

Varda's style of authorship is distinctive in that she is particularly skilled at recycling old strategies (such as her capacity to mix the codes of documentary and fiction to evoke a specific place or to tell a compelling story about marginalized people), and yet she never stops trying new ones. The "new" for Varda can mean creating a new kind of character— *Vagabond*'s utterly opaque female protagonist whose errant presence

La Chambre occupée, Paroles de squatters
(*The Occupied Room, Words of Squatters*, 2012).
© Ciné-Tamaris

sparks a multifaceted portrait of a region, for example—or venturing into a new medium, as Varda did in 2003 when she began undertaking installations for gallery exhibition. Ultimately, I hope my study reveals the continuity and the change in Varda's art-making strategies in order to refine a theory about what sets her work and her process apart.

Varda's ever-shifting profile has evolved from avant-garde precursor to the "grandmother" of the New Wave. What remains consistent is her commitment to storytelling that foregrounds isolated people in distinctive settings in both documentary and fiction films. Varda's ongoing journey reveals an artist who needs to create, who is in motion and incapable of ceasing, making do with whatever resources are available to her (including harnessing that creativity toward visual arts and installation when funds for filmmaking were scarce), remaining eminently pragmatic even when attacking new challenges.

Drawing on extensive documentation at Ciné-Tamaris, this study will highlight Varda's narrative and stylistic preoccupations, the production and exhibition histories of her work, and her shifting working methods through time. Covering Varda's entire output is impossible in a short volume, so I will focus primarily on films and art installations for which existing supporting documentation was rich enough to shed new light on Varda's work and process: the fiction films *La Pointe Courte* (1955), *Cleo* (1962), and *Vagabond* (1985); the short documentaries Varda made in the late 1950s as well as her recent feature documentaries *The Gleaners and I* (2000) and *The Beaches of Agnès* (2008); and her installations *Patatutopia* (2003), *L'île et elle* (2006), and *Des chambres en ville* (2012). While these works may seem hand-selected as artistic and critical triumphs, I would be hard-pressed to point to a failure, apart perhaps from *Les Cent et une nuits de Simon Cinéma* (*One Hundred and One Nights*, 1995), the star-studded sentimentality of which simply misfired commercially. It can nevertheless be seen as a labor of love in partial tribute to Jacques Demy that exhibited all the playful quirkiness of her overarching cinematic project, yet its heavy reliance on archival footage and extracts of others' work pushes it outside the scope of my study. My aim, grounded in archival research and focused on Varda's working methods, is to reveal both continuity and change in the long career of one of the world's most intriguing and original filmmakers.

Planning and Precision: *La Pointe Courte*

In 1954, while working as a photographer for theater legend Jean Vilar at the Théâtre National Populaire, Varda returned to her native Sète and shot her first film, *La Pointe Courte* (throughout this study, I have opted to introduce film titles in their original language before switching to the title best known to English-speaking audiences, if different, or an abbreviated version thereof, i.e., *Cleo, Vagabond, Gleaners*, etc.). So Varda's journey in the world began with a trip home, at least the home of her adolescence during the war. From this small Mediterranean fishing village, she launched a career spanning sixty years and counting, one that has never fit smoothly into the conventional categories of French film history. In the 1950s and 1960s, Varda worked in an industry populated almost exclusively by male directors, and, unlike the directors who began their careers as film critics writing for *Cahiers du cinéma*, Varda was not a voracious cinephile. As stated earlier, many film historians readily place Varda in the indistinct category of the "Left Bank," linking her with Alain Resnais, Chris Marker, Marguerite Duras, Alain Robbe-Grillet, and her late husband, Jacques Demy, because of their shared commitment to documentary filmmaking, aesthetic experimentation and the *nouveau roman*, and leftist politics. However one places her in relation to the New Wave, Varda's general aesthetic and narrative preoccupations have been fairly consistent: from *La Pointe Courte* to *The Beaches of Agnès*, Varda's work has possessed an unusual mixture of realist and experimental aesthetics, a focus on the specificity and the power of "place," and an elusive brand of self-portraiture. For the purposes of this study, I am more interested in the latter aspects of her film technique than in expanding on her formal or philosophical engagement with a well-documented moment of modernist invention.

It is not immediately clear what would have impelled someone like Varda to make a feature-length fiction film in mid-1950s France. There were few available female role models for inspiration; the only other woman directing films in France at this time was Jacqueline Audry, known especially for her literary adaptations of Colette's novels, *Gigi* (1949) and *Minne, l'ingénue libertine* (*Minne, the Libertine Ingénue*, 1950). Although Audry's films are interesting for their surprisingly complex representations of femininity and, in the case of *Olivia* (1951), a lesbian romance, Varda would not likely have been inspired by Audry's classical narratives and studio productions had she even been aware of them.

Nor did Varda have an extensive knowledge of the film industry or of film history. Instead of working her way up the hierarchy of professional film production or writing film criticism, Varda studied literature at the Sorbonne and art history at the Ecole du Louvre. Later she earned a degree in photography at the Ecole Nationale de la Cinématographie et la Photographie and then made her living shooting weddings, family photos, and advertisements before working full-time as the official photographer of the Théâtre National Populaire (TNP). Unlike other directors associated with the New Wave, Varda did not participate in France's rich postwar culture of *cinéphilie*. She was not a member of a *ciné-club* nor did she participate in the impassioned debates about realism, the film director as *auteur*, or the nature of Hollywood cinema that filled the pages of *Cahiers du cinéma* or *Positif*. She went to the cinema only once a year or so and remembers seeing Marcel Carné's *Quai des brumes* (*Daybreak*, 1938) and *Les Enfants du paradis* (*Children of Paradise*, 1945) as well as Walt Disney's *Snow White and the*

Seven Dwarfs (1937). What few films Varda had seen apparently did not please her. She told Jacques Ledoux of the Cinémathèque Royale de Belgique in a 1961 interview: "I wanted to make a film that I wanted to see. . . . I wasn't thinking at all of starting a career. I had the impression that I was going to make [only] one film" (Ledoux 1). Unlike other directors associated with the French New Wave at that time, Varda did not have a vast storehouse of images and narratives from Hollywood or European films in her head, nor did she have a network of friends in the film industry with whom she could collaborate on *La Pointe Courte*.

What skills, predilections, and commitments did Agnès Varda bring to the first film in her long and productive career? One important inspiration for the making of *La Pointe Courte* was the eponymous neighborhood in the town of Sète. Sète is a small city of forty thousand in the Languedoc-Roussillon region of southern France, far from the fashionable Côte d'Azur and even further from Paris. Like so much else in France, the filmmaking industry had always been heavily centralized, with the vast majority of personnel and production companies situated in the capital. Yet Varda chose Sète as the location for *La Pointe Courte* for several reasons. She was clearly familiar with the town, having lived there as a teenager during the war; Sète is also where she would meet Vilar, who hired her as a photographer in 1951. Not only did she have connections and close friends in the town, she loved its landscape. In a 1961 interview, Varda said, "It's the place that gave rise to the film. . . . I had the very precise sensation that there was something to discover in La Pointe Courte . . . the response to a particular problem resided in a place" (Ledoux 7–8).

The neighborhood of La Pointe Courte is a small strip of land surrounded by a large tidal pool that in the 1950s supported a vital shellfish industry. Varda uses this landscape in two ways. First, on a purely formal level, she explores the neighborhood's unusual textures and shapes created by the presence of fishing nets, ropes, small boat-building *ateliers*, steel structures, and wooden shacks. Second, she takes acute interest in the fishermen and their families: how they live and speak, their political struggles with the fisheries bureaucracy, and the rhythms of courtship, birth, marriage, and death. Yet Varda's interest in language and her love of the people and places in and around Sète cannot, in the end, fully explain the emergence of this unusual film.

In addition to the story of the villagers, Varda tells a second story, about a couple visiting La Pointe Courte from Paris. And this is one of the most startling aspects of *La Pointe Courte*: it possesses a dual structure whose narrative lines scarcely intersect. The film tells two stories, one concerning the daily difficulties and small pleasures experienced by ordinary fishermen and the other of an educated couple from Paris vacationing in the fishing village where the man was raised (thereby putting him in a slippery position as both local and visitor and making him the only potential point of narrative intersection). The couple, whom Varda does not name, is struggling through a period of *malaise* in their four-year-old marriage. Varda has often noted that she was inspired by William Faulkner's *Wild Palms*, a novel that also oscillates between two storylines, that of a convict attempting to survive a flood in 1920s Mississippi and that of an adulterous couple in the late 1930s who run away together and face poverty, an unplanned pregnancy, and a frantic attempt to procure an abortion. There are no obvious connections between the two stories in Faulkner's novel. Varda's film, likewise, braids together two stories while forging few links between them. As Neupert notes, many New Wave directors, Varda included, were unusually gifted at describing their filmmaking goals and practice. In a 1962 interview, she speaks of her film's structure, emphasizing the film's challenge to the spectator.

> I had a very clear plan for *La Pointe Courte*: it was to present two themes, that, while not really contradictory, were problems that canceled one another out when set side by side. They were, first, a couple reconsidering their relationship, and second, a village that is trying to resolve several collective problems of survival. The film was made up of chapters, so while the two themes were never mixed together there was the possibility for the spectator to oppose or superimpose them. (Neupert 59–60)

The film's movement back and forth between the two stories was thus not intended to generate meaning in and of itself. We are not, for example, asked to valorize the community over the couple or vice versa, nor are we asked to view the villagers as pathetic provincials or the couple as alienated intellectuals. Instead, the two stories, both respectful of their subjects, sit alongside one another, occasionally sharing the same space, presenting different registers of human problems. All we can say with certainty about the relationship between the two narrative threads is that the town's slow rhythms and startling landscapes seem to soften the couple's frustration with one another and render a provisional reconciliation possible.

Varda's use of style is just as unusual as her construction of narrative. *La Pointe Courte* begins with a lengthy tracking shot that moves down a small street flanked by the modest homes of fishermen before coming to rest on a fisheries inspector who stealthily observes the neighborhood. The camera weaves in and out of the small homes nearby as news of the inspector's presence travels through the community. The villagers, notably the Saldino family, resist the inspectors' attempts to search their homes and to regulate where they can fish. Down the street, a mother feeds spaghetti to her large family and cares for her sick toddler. The film's opening thus economically introduces one strand of the plot, that of the lives of the villagers, while signaling one of Varda's key stylistic strategies in the film, the use of a mobile, fluid camera that is unusually attentive to the objects, landscapes, and daily rhythms of a particular milieu. Neupert aptly sums up Varda's use of style in *La Pointe Courte*: "An elegantly restless camera, deliberate character gesture and motion, crisp use of shadow, long shot durations (the average shot length is sixteen seconds), and evocative depth of field make Varda's film one of the most unusual and beautiful motion pictures of 1950s France" (62).

In the second scene, the film introduces its other narrative line, the couple from Paris whose marriage is faltering. Although the two parts of the narrative—the daily lives of the villagers and the couple in crisis—are relatively autonomous, they are sometimes linked spatially. We catch our first glimpse of the unnamed male character (Philippe Noiret), who lives in Paris but is vacationing in his childhood home, in a characteristically dense composition. The camera weaves through hanging laundry flapping in the breeze on a sunny quay, capturing village women working and laughing. In the background of the frame, a boy passes by in a rowboat, drawing our attention to the depth and density of the frame. We see the man, Noiret, from behind and overhead as he navigates through the hanging laundry, chats with old friends, and goes to the train station to pick up his wife (Silvia Monfort), who is arriving from Paris.

Just as our introduction to the man is understated, the appearance of the woman, too, is handled in an unusual way. The man and the woman enter the frame together from the bottom right of the frame, their backs to the viewer, and then walk deep into the background and out of the frame. They continue to walk while the camera remains behind them. Access to the woman's face is thus delayed for several minutes until finally a straight-on close-up of her face occurs, followed by a high-angle moving shot of the couple walking. Such unusual stylistic choices occur throughout the film. Instead of using conventional two-shots and analytical cutting, Varda often films the backs of characters' heads, uses unexpectedly high or low angles, and employs tracking shots that are either unusually lengthy or that arc in unpredictable ways. Her compositions frequently emphasize objects (fishing nets, tools) or textures (metal and wood) over humans. Varda's style is seldom used to support narrative action in a clear, direct way, although her use of style sometimes underscores the tensions in the couple's relationship. For example, at one point during the couple's initial walk through the neighborhood, they pause on the left side of the frame, mid-ground, as a gigantic train moves slowly and menacingly along the track toward the camera. "We should separate," the wife says over the grating sound of the train during the enforced pause in their progress. More frequently, however, Varda's compositions and mobile framing sensitize the viewer to the textures and the graphic qualities of the town's landscapes. The female character is often associated with man-made metal, while the male character is related visually to more natural material, such as wood. Regardless, the film is impossible to predict as it unfolds. Tensions ebb and flow, tenderness is proferred, then refused as the couple walks through varied landscapes and settles into their rented room. Style, far from serving to support or clarify the plot, often draws attention to itself, seemingly for its own sake.

La Pointe Courte departs, then, like so many European art films, from classical causality and narrative clarity in favor of the foregrounding of its unusual structure and style. Varda specifically attributes her decision to tell two relatively isolated stories to her exposure to Bertolt Brecht's ideas while working at the Théâtre National Populaire:

> The narrative doesn't flow smoothly. It's jerky and uneven. It's almost Brechtian. At the time, I was with Jean Vilar, listening to Brecht's theories. It was the idea of Brechtian distanciation. You start listening to the couple

and then bam! Stop. You distance yourself. You see the fishermen, their social lives, the difficult economic conditions they live in, you start to get into it and then bam! Stop. Distance. Back to the couple. It could be seen as the clash between private life and social life, which can never be joined (Varda, *La Pointe Courte* DVD commentary).

Varda's acknowledged inspirations and citations—Faulkner and Brecht—situate her first film not so much in postwar French cinephilia, but instead in the broader currents of mid-century modernism, with its investment in experimental narrative forms, its refusal of spectacle and easy emotion, and its implicit challenge to viewers.

Varda's dialogue with modernism is particularly evident in the fourth scene, one of the film's richest in terms of dialogue and shot composition. Here the man and woman discuss their relationship while strolling through varied landscapes amid fishing nets, lumber, and shacks. The characters alternately express tenderness and anger. She wonders if they truly love one another or merely stay together out of habit. He expresses confidence in their love, but also frustration with her unhappiness and her pessimistic prognosis of the relationship. Compositions that place figures in several planes are the norm here; we often see the couple in the foreground or the mid-ground against a background encompassing the daily activities of villagers. In one shot, for example, the couple chats in the middle of the frame while leaning on a wooden structure. Nets hanging on wooden sticks surround the couple, while in the background cyclists traverse the frame laterally. Close-ups of the couple occasionally show their heads close together, but feature them looking in different directions. Such shots evoke Picasso's paintings that simultaneously show a face frontally and in profile; they also anticipate the shots in Bergman's *Persona* that feature the heads of Bibi Andersson and Liv Ullmann, strangely fused yet looking in different directions. Another shot, this time taken from behind the wooden structure, features the couple in the foreground with a rocky path extending out into the pond; the couple moves into mid-frame and faces the water, backs to the camera, now separated by nets and the rocky path. The shot composition, with its clear graphic division of the figures of the man and woman by the rocky path, suggests discord, and yet it is during this shot that the man says, "But I won't want to live any other way than with you; we chose one another." The viewer is kept off guard during such moments. Indeed, throughout *La Pointe Courte*, it is often difficult to anticipate the couple's meandering movements and the fluctuating tone of their exchanges. The film is startling not only for its setting, structure, and style, but also for the couple's conversations. Throughout the film, the man and the woman walk and talk, analyzing with both bitterness and tenderness their marriage of four years. Indeed, their meandering conversations replace the dramatic events of a more traditional film. Apart from the woman's arrival in Sète and the couple's departure at the end of the film, very little actually happens to them. They walk, talk, watch the jousting tournament, and prepare to return to Paris. This relative lack of causal, decisive, or dramatic events in the film was quite intentional. Varda later said:

> I was irritated because in the few films that I had seen, it always seemed to me that the films were preoccupied with dramas, crises, things that happened; for example . . . we see stories where the couples divorce or fight or rather a lover arrives or rather one of the two dies. I find that too many things always happen. . . . we never pay attention to the things between those two moments when the people no longer love one another quite enough but you see that they still love one another. . . . this is the case with the couple of *La Pointe Courte* which is a couple on the way down, but it's still a couple (Ledoux 8).

This attempt to explore the "in-between" moments in the life of a couple during long, meandering walks through a distinctive and decisively shot landscape is something that links Varda to other European modernist filmmakers in the 1950s and 1960s. A year earlier, Rossellini's *Viaggio in Italia* (*Journey to Italy*, 1954) had told the story of a middle-aged couple whose marriage has soured due to resentment and boredom, while Resnais's *Hiroshima mon amour* (1959) featured protracted conversations between a man and a woman in the bars and streets of Hiroshima. Jean-Luc Godard's *A bout de souffle* (*Breathless*, 1960), *Une femme est une femme* (*A Woman Is a Woman*, 1961), and *Le Mépris* (*Contempt*, 1963) each contains extended scenes in which couples flirt and argue. Antonioini's *L'Eclisse* (*The Eclipse*, 1962) opens in the middle of one couple's breakup, pairs the woman with a new man, but then concludes with the disappearance of the protagonists from the plot altogether. Prior to that, *L'Avventura* (1960) eliminated one of its female protagonists early on, formed a new couple with the missing woman's boyfriend and her best friend, and then concluded with the probable dissolution of the new couple. This way of treating romantic relationships—foregrounding tension, inertia, repetition, and uncertainty—seems a particularly significant feature of modernist European cinema of the 1950s and early 1960s. The journey of such couples is neither an inexorable drive toward union nor a clear rupture, but instead an uneven and unpredictable experience often characterized by abrupt tonal shifts, dialogue that trails off or is opaque, and lingering uncertainty as to the couple's future at the film's conclusion. Such couples, sometimes highly verbal and sometimes frustratingly silent, seem very far indeed from both classical Hollywood and conventional European cinema of the 1950s.

Varda's couple is distinctive, even in the context of European art cinema, and I argue that it is derived in large part from her direction of the performances of Noiret and Monfort. These performances are intriguing both for their departure from the highly polished, professional, and psychologically realistic performance styles in 1950s "quality" French cinema and for Varda's rare mixing of de-dramatized and naturalistic acting styles. Experienced theater actors, Noiret and Monfort deliver literary, even overtly poetic dialogue in a relatively flat fashion, with minimal modulation in volume or tone. Such austere performances result in the generation of little emotion in the viewers and instead encourage us to analyze the couple's dilemma and try to understand the causes of their frustration with one another. Jean Vilar, director of the Théâtre National Populaire and Varda's employer, was at this time also aiming for a style of acting that avoided the extremes of both the actor's complete "disappearance" into the character and a radical Brechtian distanciation between actor and character (Loyer 171). While Varda has not pointed to Vilar's acting philosophy as a particular influence on *La Pointe Courte*, it seems likely that her direction of her actors was at least partly influenced by her exposure to the performances she saw at the TNP. She certainly had a specific style in mind for the performances of Noiret and Monfort. In her 1994 autobiography, Varda explains that she wanted her actors to sound as if they were reading their lines, not enacting them. "I wanted the actors neither to act nor to express feelings, [only] to be there and to say their dialogue as if they were reading it. In fact, I was thinking of the narrators of oriental performances [and] of Egyptian sculptures of kneeling couples or of pairs of recumbent sculptures in dark churches" (Varda, *Varda par Agnès*, 44). Varda's goal in representing the couple was clearly not to create the impression of verisimilitude. She said as much in a 1961 interview: "I wanted [the couple] to seem artificial [*faux*]. I didn't want people to identify with them. So I wanted them to have a certain tone, to say things in a literary fashion, a bit stereotyped, things that in other circumstances would be said differently. It is obvious that a couple explaining themselves to one another does not speak like that. I wanted this fabricated [way of speaking] to be represented theatrically, if you like. It is a theater of the couple" (Ledoux 13). Varda was aiming specifically for an impression of rigidity, of stasis. "As I was a photographer, I like things that do not move. I really like portraits . . . *La Pointe Courte* is not well edited. It moves from one place to another without continuity. So, because there is no continuity, there was no obligation to have a lot of movement. Basically, it's like a recitative. I see it a bit like an opera; people plant themselves and they sing. They talk. I didn't want it to seem at all real" (Ledoux 14). The hieratic poses of Noiret and Monfort and their highly literary dialogue were quite unusual in the 1950s. Not everyone understood or appreciated these performances, but Varda was unwittingly in step with some of the most radical filmmakers of her day, Jacques Tati and Robert Bresson among them, who in different ways, both from one another and from Varda, also created de-dramatized performances.

The performances Varda elicited were significant not only for their overt artificiality and absence of affect, but also for their juxtaposition with the naturalistic performances of the villagers. The villagers, played by nonprofessional actors who were actually residents of La Pointe Courte, possess relatively mobile faces and bodies with which they express conventional facsimiles of emotions such as affection and grief.

Moreover, in contrast to the couple, the villagers use vernacular language. "We've already shat out half our crap," a middle-aged woman says to her husband in reference to their life trajectory. It is difficult to find precursors for Varda's particular juxtaposition of an austere acting style from her professional actors with a vibrant, naturalistic style of acting from the nonprofessionals. It is as if Varda had been inspired by the workers' performances in *Ladri di biciclette* (*Bicycle Thieves*, 1948) and

Varda working with a nonprofessional actor on *La Pointe Courte* (1955). © Ciné-Tamaris

had also anticipated Antonioni's alienated couples in *L'Avventura* and *The Eclipse*. This mixture of acting styles is similar to the postneorealist cinema of Rossellini, notably *Stromboli* (1950) and *Journey to Italy*, films that also juxtapose urban northern intellectuals with southern rural laborers. And like both of those Italians working in the wake of neorealism, Varda's loyalties were divided; she is essentially a creature of the North, but she can claim some affiliation to (certainly affinity for) the southern community. She hovers between local and tourist. It is hard to argue, however, for a direct neorealist influence, since Varda was unfamiliar with the work of Rossellini or any other Italian directors at this stage of her career. Instead Varda's immersion in modernism (in both the literary and the visual arts) and her exposure to Vilar's theatrical experiments appear to have shaped her audacious direction of performance.

Despite the apparent unlikelihood of Varda's venturing into filmmaking, much less engaging in unusual experiments in shot composition and acting, she had long immersed herself in art and literature of all kinds. Upon graduating from high school in Paris, Varda lived with friends in an apartment near Pigalle and did little else but read modernist fiction and poetry for an entire year (Varda, personal interview with the author,

2013). As a young woman in Paris, Varda surrounded herself with artists from Sète, notably the Schlengel sisters. Andrée Schlengel, an engraver, eventually married TNP director Jean Vilar. Valentine (Linou) Schlengel, Varda's closest adolescent friend, studied fine arts in Montpellier and became a ceramicist and sculptor. Varda speaks of Linou Schlengel's influence on her at length in her 1994 autobiography: "She knew how to take the time to look and shared with me her quest for beauty in forms as varied as they were unexpected. From the sarcophagi at the Louvre to the leprous walls of the suburbs, from a piece of fruit cut open to the abstractions of Nicolas de Stael, from a pebble to a jewel" (Varda, *Varda par Agnès*, 22). By the time she was in her early twenties, Varda had a network of friends, working artists, who lived near or with her in the 14th arrondissement in Paris. Although Varda may have been uneducated about the procedures of filmmaking when she set out to make *La Pointe Courte*, she had long conceived of herself as an artist capable of launching ambitious projects.

Varda was also entirely at home with the principles of visual composition and literary experimentation. Varda's taste for theater, literature, and painting—she has often evoked her specific predilection for Renaissance painting, the work of Picasso, and the literature of Faulkner, Dos Passos, and Woolf—were wide-ranging and shaped by her formal schooling as well as her community of artist friends in Paris. She wrote in her autobiography, "I loved the arts; the only magazine I bought was *Beaux Arts* and the Cubist revolution seemed much more important to me than the Russian one" (Varda, *Varda par Agnès*, 38). She used the resources and skills she had at hand: a modest inheritance from her father, a loan from her mother, the assistance of loyal friends, generous actors at the TNP, and her experience as a photographer. But one also must assume that the postwar climate of France, with its burgeoning arts scene designed to encourage nonprofessionals to participate in theater, music, *ciné-clubs*, or book clubs, along with the ongoing vitality of modernism in the visual and literary arts, created an atmosphere in which Varda's experimentation seemed not only feasible but essential. Varda's personal energy and insatiable desire to experiment, it would seem, have fueled her career from the beginning, but external forces in French culture have also shaped her career. We will explore some of these in the section on Varda's second feature, *Cleo from 5 to 7*.

The importance of *La Pointe Courte* for French film history lies as much in its mode of production as in its unusual plot structure, dense shot compositions, and its mélange of acting styles. By the mid-1950s, the French film industry had long been characterized by the presence of many small, independent production companies that managed to make only a few films per year, but *La Pointe Courte*'s mode of production was extremely artisanal even by French standards, notably because Varda produced the film herself. She formed her own production company in August 1954 and named it Tamaris (tamarisk) in reference to the ornamental tree found in the Mediterranean. The film's budget was seven million old francs (or $14,000) (Neupert 57) at a time when the typical film budget was closer to 150 million, with coproductions costing

Varda shooting *La Pointe Courte* (1955).
© Ciné-Tamaris

as much as 250 million francs (Crisp 86). Having no access to traditional sources of financing, Varda funded the production using a small inheritance she received from her father and a loan from her mother, while the cast and crew worked for shares in a cooperative (Neupert 57). The residents of Sète who played the roles of the villagers donated their time and effort to the production. The size of the budget and the production's cooperative structure were thus highly unusual, as was Varda's decision to film on location, far from the centralized film studios of Boulogne, outside Paris. The shoot took place from August 10 to September 31, 1954. Varda had done a considerable amount of scouting beforehand and had taken many photographs that would provide inspiration for shot compositions: "[C]ertain photos that I had taken while scouting were so interesting . . . for their framing or as atmosphere, that I tried to find on the shoot the exact conditions of décor or lighting or the type of characters" (Ledoux 69–70). The cast and crew lived together in an inexpensive rented house near a Shell oil refinery that was located ten kilometers from Sète. Varda slept in the garage next to the used car she had purchased for the shoot. The only professional actors in the film were Noiret and Monfort, who were on vacation from the TNP; all the other characters were played by the generous inhabitants of Sète. The cinematographer, Louis Stein, at thirty-two the oldest member of the crew, had already worked as a cameraman for Jacques Becker, Yves Allégret, and André Cayette. The film was shot silent because Varda could not afford synchronous sound recording, but a sound recorder was on hand to record ambient sound and voice. The sound recorder often malfunctioned, however, so Varda had to reconstruct the dialogue track in Paris (Mardiguian). Carlos Vilardebo, who had worked as an assistant director and would become a director himself eventually, helped Varda with all manner of practical things, such as the rental of the camera and lights; his wife, Jane Vilardebo, served as script supervisor, production secretary, and daily transporter of rushes to the train bound for Paris. The rushes were screened at a local cinema, the Colisée, where the completed film would be shown a year later to the townspeople. Varda's childhood friend, Valentine Schlengel, served as artistic advisor, while Bienvenida Llorca, Varda's friend and neighbor, came down from Paris to cook and do laundry for the crew. Llorca served as an extra in the film as well, hanging up laundry on the quay.[1] The cast and crew worked from 7:00 AM to 8:00 PM each day and at the beginning of the shoot worked for twenty-eight days in a row without a break (Varda, Ciné-Tamaris Archive, *La Pointe Courte*).

Once the film was shot, Varda returned to Paris and started looking for an editor who would be willing to work for shares in the cooperative instead of for cash. She was advised to contact Alain Resnais, already known for his short documentaries on art and artists, notably *Van Gogh* (1948), *Guernica* (1950), and *Gauguin* (1950). Resnais had also codirected, with Chris Marker, *Les Statues meurent aussi* (*Statues Also Die*, 1953), a film whose critique of French colonialism and the commercialization of African art caused it to be banned in France for fifteen years after it was made (Wilson 22). Varda asked Resnais to consider editing the film in the fall of 1954, some months before Resnais would begin working on *Night and Fog*. Resnais hesitated repeatedly before agreeing to work with Varda, in part because he felt that her aesthetic pursuits resembled too closely his own goals (Varda, *Varda par Agnès*, 46). But he eventually accepted the job and, over the course of several months, whittled ten hours of rushes down to one and a half. Varda expressed gratitude in her autobiography that Resnais had retained the film's slow pace instead of imposing a new, faster rhythm on it (Ibid.).

When it came time to distribute *La Pointe Courte*, Varda's challenges were not over. In 1954, Bastide reports, when Varda created her production company, she had registered it with the Centre National de la Cinémathographie (CNC) as a producer of short films because she did not have the required capital to register as a feature filmmaker (Bastide, "*La Pointe Courte*," 31–36). Varda wrote to the CNC in August 1954 to request authorization to transform her status from a producer of short films to a producer of features. The CNC proposed two solutions: increase Tamaris's start-up capital from one million francs to five million francs or join forces with a coproducer already authorized to produce feature films. Neither solution was possible for Varda, so the company retained its status as a maker of short films, which made the legal theatrical distribution of Varda's feature-length *La Pointe Courte* impossible.

The film's exhibition thus took place largely in the noncommercial sector of the *ciné-club*. For a film that never received a traditional theatrical release, *La Pointe Courte* generated an extraordinary amount of attention, largely positive. This attention was initiated by critic André Bazin, to whom Varda had shown *La Pointe Courte* upon the advice of Resnais. Bazin liked the film and advised Varda to do several things: organize a private screening of the film at a cinema in Cannes during the 1955 Cannes Film Festival; advertise the screening in *Film Français*, the film industry's trade paper; and invite critics and industry professionals to the projection (Varda, "Hommage à André Bazin"). Varda took Bazin's advice and benefited from the numerous positive reviews that emerged from the screening, including those written by Bazin himself.

Bazin saw in *La Pointe Courte* a kind of personal filmmaking that corresponded precisely to a notion of cinema for which he had been advocating since the late 1940s in his film criticism and lectures. Bazin argued for a modern cinema that was innovative in terms of its style and storytelling strategies, yet designed for a broader audience than that of the 1920s avant-garde. In his reviews of *La Pointe Courte*, Bazin approvingly distinguishes *La Pointe Courte* from the 1920s avant-garde of "formal audacity" and "retarded surrealism" (*La Cinématographie française*). The film's narrative "possesses the nuances and slow development of a novel" and the plot displays an "unexpected and necessary relationship . . . [to its] geographical and human landscape" (Bazin, *La Cinématographie française*). Bazin again distanced *La Pointe Courte* from the 1920s avant-garde a few months later in the pages of *Cahiers du cinéma*, stating that the film is "really far from the formal research and the negation of subject that characterized the avant-garde of 1925 ("Petit Journal"). Instead, Bazin approvingly notes, *La Pointe Courte* "is akin to an intimate diary or, better yet, to a story in the first person that one put, for the sake of discretion, into the third person." Well known for his appreciation of Italian Neorealist cinema, Bazin gave the highest compliment to Varda by linking her film to Visconti's *La Terra Trema* (1948), another realist film set in a southern European fishing town; however, he notes, Varda's work is distinctive in its separation of the couple's story from that of the community (Bazin, *La Cinématographie française*). In an article titled "Agnès and Roberto," Bazin again associated Varda with Italian Neorealism by linking *La Pointe Courte* to Roberto Rossellini's *Journey to Italy*.[2] A few months later, Bazin wrote again in *Parisien Libéré* of Varda's particular brand of realism, noting its combination of simplicity and stylization: "Everything in it is simple and natural and, at the same time, shorn and composed" ("La Pointe courte"). Bazin was also struck by the film's mode of production. In the same essay, he wrote that the very existence of the film was "miraculous" and that one would have to go back to Cocteau's *Le Sang d'un poète* (*Blood of a Poet*, 1930) to find a film "as free from all commercial contingencies in its conception." Varda's unusual decision to form a cooperative among the cast and crew was remarked upon by several film critics, as was the film's low budget. Another critic compared *La Pointe Courte* favorably to Max Ophüls's *Lola Montès* (1955), which was made the same year, but for sixty times the cost (Davay).

Although most of the film reviews of *La Pointe Courte* were positive, critics occasionally registered disapproval of Varda's aesthetic choices. Georges Charensol, editor of *Nouvelles Littéraires* and Cannes insider, found Varda's careful compositions "gratuitous" and objected to the film's dual structure. Critic and filmmaker François Truffaut (who had yet to release a feature himself) found the shots "a little too 'framed'" ("un peu trop 'cadrés'"), the dialogue too theatrical and "laborious," and Varda's direction of Monfort and Noiret too "uncertain." Truffaut's review is oddly malicious; he muses that Varda's resemblance to her leading man is not accidental and then facetiously expresses anxiety that he has spent too much time writing about the film's form over its content because "it was the surest way to avoid writing the stupidities expected by the very cerebral director." Jacques Siclier also denigrated Varda for her supposedly excessive intelligence: "So much intellectualism in a young woman is distressing" (Varda, *Varda par Agnès*, 40).

These few dissenting voices aside, the film received enthusiastic reviews and remained in the public attention for quite some time after its initial screening in Cannes. *La Pointe Courte* was screened once more in Paris on June 12, 1955, at the Cinéma du Panthéon, an important art house founded in 1930 by Pierre Braunberger, who had been in the audience with André Bazin at the private screening the previous fall. Next the film was shown at the Studio Parnasse on every Tuesday evening in January 1956. The Studio Parnasse was a particularly advantageous venue for *La Pointe Courte*. It was known to have some of the best film programming in Paris and its director, Jean-Louis Chéray, hosted lively discussions after the screenings. Eleven thousand viewers saw the film at the Studio Parnasse, including François Truffaut (again), Chris Marker, Marguerite Duras, and Natalie Sarraute, another *nouveau roman* adherent who would become one of Varda's friends (Varda, *Varda par Agnès*). The film was also screened in Sète at the Colisée cinema in 1955 and every ten years thereafter. Until its 1994 release on video and its 2007 release on DVD, the film in which Varda learned to "take an interest" in the world she documented was nearly impossible to see. Nevertheless, *La Pointe Courte* had an outsized impact on film culture due to its unusual combination of realism and stylization, which appealed to influential tastemakers such as André Bazin, and as a result of its independent, low-budget mode of production, which would serve as a model for New Wave filmmakers in the late 1950s and beyond.

Structure and Digression: The Early Short Documentaries

After Varda made her first feature, it was not at all obvious that a long, successful career as a filmmaker lay ahead of her. She continued to work as a photographer for the Théâtre National Populaire and traveled to China in 1957 for a photography project. Varda also made three short documentaries in the late 1950s: *Ô saisons, Ô chateaux* (1957), *L'Opéra-Mouffe* (1958), and *Du côté de la côte* (1958). The decision to make short films might seem odd, given that she had already made a critically celebrated feature-length film. In fact, making shorts was a logical and highly beneficial move on her part. From the 1940s through the 1960s in France, short films were ubiquitous, initially because they were quite profitable. A 1940 law had outlawed the double feature and put in place a mechanism whereby 3 percent of the gross receipts of a full program (the short plus the feature film) would go to the producer of the short film (Porcile 15). The practice continued after the war, when the typical program consisted of a ten-minute newsreel, a short documentary, a trailer of the following week's feature, and finally the feature. Most short films were documentaries and fell into one of several well-developed subgenres: the scientific film, the film about art, and the pedagogical film, which could focus on anything from coal mining to barge construction.

Not only was the short film lucrative, it enjoyed an extraordinary aesthetic richness in postwar France. Thanks in part to the *ciné-club* movement and the active critical community, directors of short documentaries were seen as *auteurs*. Jean Painlevé had been making surrealism-infused documentaries about wildlife since the 1920s. Jean Vigo's *A propos de Nice* (1930) had shown that one could document specific places and social realities while exploring avant-garde aesthetics. Georges Franju's *Le Sang des bêtes* (*Blood of the Beasts*, 1949) is both a pedagogical film focusing on a specific work environment, the slaughterhouse, as well as a poetic portrait of a working-class neighborhood. Alain Resnais had been making short films about art since the late 1940s and had become well known for his documentary about the Holocaust, *Night and Fog* (1955). Also contributing to the richness of the documentary short in postwar France was the emergence of audacious and respected producers such as Anatole Dauman, who gave Varda the opportunity to make *Du côté de la côte* (1958). Dauman's Argos Films produced Resnais's *Night and Fog* and *Hiroshima mon amour* (1959), Marker's *Lettre de Sibérie* (*Letter from Siberia*, 1957), Jean Rouch and Edgar Morin's *Chronique d'un été* (*Chronicle of a Summer*, 1961), and Marker's *La Jetée* (1962). Varda's choice to make short films not only made economic sense, but it allowed her to join the ranks of respected directors creating aesthetically innovative short films. It also allowed her to play the part of the tourist, literally plotting out her productions using guidebooks, a role that aptly characterized the next phase in her journey as a peripatetic filmmaker.

Ô saisons, Ô chateaux (1957)

Varda's first short film, *Ô saisons, Ô chateaux*, was commissioned by the Office National du Tourisme (ONT, National Tourism Board) and designed to promote the castles of France's Loire Valley. For this project, Resnais, who had edited *La Pointe Courte*, recommended Varda to producer Pierre Braunberger, another risk-taking producer. Braunberger had been active in the film industry since the late 1920s, having produced Jean Renoir's *La Chienne* (1931) and *Partie de campagne* (*A Day in the Country*, 1936), Jean Rouch's *Moi, un noir* (1958), and Resnais's short films on art. Braunberger recommended Varda to the ONT, which in turn offered the commission to Varda. Varda certainly understood the value of making a professional connection with Braunberger but did not feel an immediate connection to the film's subject. Nevertheless, she departed on a scouting trip with two tools in hand: her Rolleiflex camera

Varda scouting locations for *Ô saisons,
Ô chateaux* (1957). © Ciné-Tamaris

and Hachette's Guide Bleu for the region. The tourist guide served as
a tool for planning her scouting visits, but more than this it inspired the
structure of her film.

Ô saisons, Ô chateaux presents an inventory of castles whose architectural features are explained by a voice-over, voiced by Danièle
Delorme, a well-known actress who had played *ingénue* roles in Jacqueline Audry's *Gigi* (1949) and *Minne, l'ingénue libertine* (1950). The
film initially purports to offer a celebratory history of French royal architecture that moves from bulky defensive fortresses to the glories of
the Renaissance, but in fact, as Varda has stated, the architectural history

takes up only eight minutes of the twenty-two-minute film (Varda, *Varda par Agnès*, 74). In the other fourteen minutes, Varda departs from the architectural chronology in witty and surprising ways. For example, a shot of a fortress gives way to a shot of a model wearing a fur hat and carrying a white fur muff, and then to a shot containing animal heads mounted on a wall, suggesting a link between beautiful women and trophy animals on display. No obvious explanation is provided for the sudden appearance of fashion models in the film; they seem at first merely to be a visual joke on Varda's part. Later, when the models appear once again, they stroll slowly around the terraces of Chambord wearing colorful, formal *haute couture* gowns borrowed from designer Jacques Heim. The models in their elegant gowns evoke the leisurely lives and decorative functions of aristocratic women. In a series of long takes, Varda shows us the fabric of the gorgeous gowns fluttering in the breeze, but ultimately she is more interested in the castles' caretakers. The voice-over tells us, "François I probably never imagined that the 365 rooms, complete with fireplaces, would be neither furnished nor inhabited except during brief Court visits. Or that those who would enjoy the palace most would be three generations of caretakers." A caretaker standing proudly in front of Chambord holds his family photo while the voice-over exhorts us to pay honor to this dynasty: "Meet the caretakers' branch of the Chambord family."

A pattern is established, and the film then alternates between an architectural history and digressions through the decorative, the apparently marginal, or the half-forgotten. These detours take many forms: the stylized movements of gardeners set to a jazz soundtrack, an encounter with the last remaining trained stonecutter, a clip from the 1908 film *L'assassinat du Duc de Guise* (André Calmettes and Charles Le Bargy) during the section on the Chateau de Blois, and images of the work of an amateur painter Varda met on a scouting trip who painted only on Sundays and only the castles of the Loire (Varda, *Varda par Agnès*, 74). Such passages supply humor, variety, and even an alternative way of looking at history in the sense that apparently marginal actors (workers, notably) are given as much attention as the royal figures that inhabited the chateaux of the Loire. As she did with *La Pointe Courte* and with later films such as *Documenteur* (1981), *Vagabond*, and *The Gleaners and I*, Varda asks viewers to look closely and admiringly at the lives of apparently ordinary people. With her first documentary, then, Varda established an organizational structure she would use again and again: create a clear structure, whether a travelogue, a typology, or an inventory of some kind, and then supplement it with digressive, witty, or more personal material. The film was well-received critically; it was selected for the 1958 Cannes Film Festival and the Festival de Tours, a festival of short films where she met her future husband Jacques Demy, and screened in theaters before an adaptation of Molière's *Bourgeois gentilhomme* (Jean Meyer, 1958).

Du côté de la côte (1958)

Varda made another short documentary for the ONT, *Du côté de la côte* (1958), produced by Anatole Dauman and designed to promote the Riviera as a tourist destination. As with *Ô saisons, Ô chateaux*, Varda enjoyed a more professional mode of production; both films were shot with a professional crew, in 35mm and in Eastman color. For *Du côté de la côte* Varda was granted eight weeks to shoot a thirty-minute film. But she nevertheless found it challenging: how to construct a compelling documentary about a region that connoted glamour and superficial tourism? Jean Vigo had already documented the poetic and the exploitative aspects of Riviera tourism with *A propos de Nice* in 1930. In 1952, Paul Paviot made *Saint-Tropez, devoir de vacances*, which likewise took a gently ironic look at the desires and habits of tourists in the south of France. And Roger Vadim's *Et Dieu créa . . . la femme* (*And God Created Woman*, 1955) created a durable link between the Côte d'Azur, Brigitte Bardot, and eroticism. How to say something fresh about this region? Varda opted for a heterogeneous and witty pastiche that both documents the "exotic" places of the Côte d'Azur and questions its status as a kind of Garden of Eden.

Once again, Varda turned to an Hachette Guide Bleu as her inspiration, and once again she established a strong central structure for *Du côté de la côte*. The guidebook's litany of places and names provided her central idea for the film: "I chose [to focus on] exoticism: the Russian Church of Nice, the mosque of Fréjus, the exotic gardens and private villas." As she did with her first documentary, Varda fills her film with digressions, moving from architecture to sunbathers to sun hats on the basis of associational links between words or images. Ultimately, *Du côté de la côte* suggests that the most beautiful parts of the Côte d'Azur, the private estates and beaches, are only available to the rich. But the film's witty asides, with their playful logic, set the dominant tone and give the film its charm. Just as with *Ô saisons, Ô chateaux*, Varda found a way to work within the constraints associated with a commissioned project, yet put her personal stamp on the film.

After she completed *Du côté de la côte*, she was still absorbed enough by the topic of the Côte d'Azur to create a follow-up project in 1961, a small book containing stills and text from her film as well as additional archival material relating to the region, including reproductions of film stills, prints, and paintings found at film archives and the Bibliothèque National de France (Varda, *La Côte d'Azur*). As we will see with *Cléo from 5 to 7* and *The Gleaners and I*, Varda often extends her film texts by creating related works on film and in other media and, in the era of the DVD, through her unusually elaborate extras, or "boni," as she calls them.[3] Two other positive developments emerged as a result of making the film: Varda was linked once again with Alain Resnais, this time in terms of their films' exhibition: *Du côté de la côte* was paired with Resnais's *Hiroshima mon amour* in the theaters, where it was seen by two million viewers (Bastide, "Agnès Varda," 77). Varda's second documentary short was also shown at the Festival de Tours.

L'Opéra-Mouffe (1958)

Between the making of *Ô saisons, Ô chateaux* and *Du côté de la côte*, Varda made another short documentary, this one self-produced. Upon first glance, *L'Opéra-Mouffe* (1958) seems quite different from the two commissioned documentaries. For one thing, she would not assume the role of the tourist exactly, but instead would transpose her own quotidian experience of the final weeks of pregnancy to a neighborhood not too far from her own. The initial motivation for the film, a portrait of the rue Mouffetard in Paris, came not from a tourism office, but from Jacques Ledoux, esteemed curator of the Cinémathèque royale de Belgique. In 1957, Ledoux invited Varda to submit a work for his program of experimental films at the 1958 World's Fair in Brussels. Inspired by this invitation, she set out to prepare the film. Varda made the film while pregnant with her first child, Rosalie, and wanted to convey something of the contradictory feelings of hope for the new life she was bringing into the world and her despair about the poverty she saw around her (Varda, Introduction to *L'Opéra-Mouffe*, *Varda Tous Courts* DVD). Varda knew rue Mouffetard well, a market street in the 5th arrondisement of Paris, notable in the 1950s both for its produce stands and for its unsanitary, cramped living quarters.[4] She had already begun collaborating on a book and record project about rue Mouffetard with singer-songwriter Jean-Pierre Suc, a friend from Sète, who ran a cabaret on rue Mouffetard (Varda, *Varda par Agnès*, 114). That project never came to fruition, but Varda used the photographs she had already taken of people living on the street as a springboard for *L'Opéra-Mouffe*.

When it came time to shoot the film, she borrowed a 16mm camera and took a folding chair to the rue Mouffetard, put the camera on a tripod, and stood on the chair to shoot the life of the street. The film was shot silent; there is no dialogue or voice-over, only Georges Delerue's music and brief passages of lyrics placed at the beginning of each section. The film contains three types of images: the footage Varda filmed of people in the street, usually elderly, poor, and alcoholic; a narrative fragment about a woman frolicking nude with one lover and then another; and images of vegetable or animal life that are rendered abstract through Varda's compositions and Delerue's music.

L'Opéra-Mouffe is much more personal than the commissioned documentaries. A title at the beginning of the film announces that this is the "filmed journal of a pregnant woman," and the first few images of the film are of a nude, pregnant body against a black background. The film thus is framed both in words and in images by Varda's pregnant state. But a shock cut interrupts any romanticized reverie the viewer might have experienced about the link between femininity and fecundity: a shot of a pregnant belly is followed by a shot of a huge pumpkin. A knife cuts into the pumpkin and a hand scrapes out the seeds, suggesting the violence of childbirth or even an abortion. (Fifteen years later, Varda would figure among the 343 "*salopes*"—sluts—who signed a 1973 manifesto calling for legalized abortion.) At the end of the film, an obviously exhausted, perhaps catatonic, pregnant woman walks along the street,

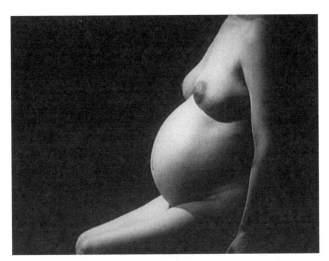

Representing the subjective experience
of a pregnant woman in *L'Opéra-Mouffe* (1958).
© Ciné-Tamaris

while potatoes fall out of her shopping bag, one by one. Mysteriously, she buys, and then slowly eats, flowers. The film thus offers, among other things, a startling and occasionally disturbing poetic exploration of the imagination of the pregnant woman. It is also a portrait of the river of humanity moving along the street; we see witty montages of gossiping shoppers as well as the careworn people who shop and live in the neighborhood. This emphasis on the movement of people along a crowded street was quite intentional: "I wanted it to be in the spirit in which Cartier-Bresson sometimes does his photos, but in a swarm; so as to convey a sensation of swarming so intense that one couldn't isolate the shots. Moreover there are shots that are less than one second long" (Ledoux 73).

Unlike *Rue Mouffetard* (Jacques Krier, 1959), the more traditional documentary made the following year, Varda's film refrains from offering solutions to the problems of poverty, alcoholism, and overcrowding. Krier's documentary, made for television and narrated by journalist and television producer Etienne Lalou, employs an expository documentary approach that combines an authoritative, explanatory voice-over, numerous man-in-the-street interviews, alarming statistics about the poor living conditions, and a reassuring round-table discussion with sociologists filmed in a studio. Varda's film, in contrast, creates a more impressionistic, dreamlike film that summons a dark vision of pregnancy, erotic pleasure, and hardship.

There are obvious differences between *L'Opéra-Mouffe* and the other two short documentaries she made in the 1950s, but Varda's similar working methods and structuring principles can be seen in all three films. As with the commissioned documentaries, *L'Opéra-Mouffe* employs a clear structure, but the structure bears a more personal stamp. There was no Hachette Guide to inspire Varda as she constructed her tour of rue Mouffetard, a place designated by French health officials in the 1950s as an *îlot insalubre* (unsanitary slum). Nevertheless, she created a structure once again, this time based on the people and places she encountered while researching the film. She wrote her own "guide" to the neighborhood, as it were, by creating a kind of photo album containing still images of the

Hardship on the rue Mouffetard,
L'Opéra-Mouffe (1958). © Ciné-Tamaris

inhabitants as well as informational or poetic captions, some of which became song lyrics, scrawled in the margins of the notebook. The notebook is organized into categories such as "food," "bums" [*clochards*], and "wine," categories that Varda would eventually retain in the film in the form of titles. Thouvenal rightly notes that *L'Opéra-Mouffe* possesses the structure of an inventory, most likely influenced by the lengthy French literary tradition of the poetic inventory in the work of Jacques Prévert and Georges Perec (191). In moving from the notebook to the film, Varda changed some of the categories. For example, "the bums" was changed to "dearly departed" because many of the alcoholic homeless people she photographed at the beginning of the project had died during the winter of 1958. Not only does the film retain the structure of the notebook, it retains several of the images of these homeless people pasted into the preproduction planning notebook. Whether Varda was working on a commissioned film or a self-produced film, whether she had a big or small budget, whether she had lots of time or very little time to make the film, she used the same strategies: a strong structure imposed from the outset that has elements of a typology and a travelogue. Digressions or supplemental elements, whether ironic, tender, or humorous, enrich that structure as the film develops.

L'Opéra-Mouffe was shown at festivals and in *ciné-clubs*, where it was well-received. The film was awarded a prize at the Brussels World's Fair in 1958 by the Fédération Internationale des Ciné-clubs (International Federation of Ciné-clubs). Amos Vogel, the influential director of the first New York Film Festival and a tireless promoter of experimental cinema, distributed *L'Opéra-Mouffe* in the United States through Cinema 16, his film society. Alternative exhibition spaces have always played an important role in Varda's career. The phenomenon of the *ciné-club* bears close examination, for it played a significant role in creating an audience for all different kinds of films, including European art cinema and classical Hollywood titles. Indeed, Varda's second feature, *Cleo from 5 to 7*, benefited enormously from the support of a specific *ciné-club*.

Cultivating the New Wave Spectator: *Cleo from 5 to 7*

In 1961, when Varda began to make her second feature-length fiction film, *Cleo from 5 to 7*, the conditions under which she worked were different from those of her first feature. This time, she shot her film three years into the New Wave, when producers were accustomed to funding low-budget features by the likes of Truffaut, Godard, and Resnais. In contrast to her first feature's production, this time she had financial backing from Georges de Beauregard, the producer of Godard's *Breathless* and Demy's *Lola*. She was also able to employ professional actors and had a larger, professional crew. Her budget was still small ($64,000) but typical of a New Wave budget (Neupert 333). She shot on location, just as she had in Sète, but this time she shifted her setting to Paris, the center of French filmmaking. Like other New Wave filmmakers, Varda shot in apartments, streets, cafes, stores, and parks, combining formal experimentation with the texture of everyday life in the early 1960s.

Just as she had in the making of *La Pointe Courte*, Varda chose to write an original screenplay for *Cleo from 5 to 7* instead of adapting a novel or play. She also continued to experiment with form and style, but she developed some new storytelling strategies this time. Whereas her first feature wove together two disparate narratives, her second feature experimented with duration, creating the impression of real time in telling a story about one character. Moreover, in 1961, in con-

Varda shooting *Cleo from 5 to 7* (1962)
on location in Paris. © Ciné-Tamaris

trast to the mid-1950s, Varda was part of the filmmaking community and the partner of another important filmmaker, Jacques Demy. Still, in a 1961 interview, she spoke of having lost something in the move from first-time filmmaker to experienced director of both fiction and documentary films: "The fact that I didn't know anyone [while making *La Pointe Courte*] meant that I worked in a spirit of total freedom. . . . I really had the impression that there was no other way to express what I wanted to express, but especially that that was how I needed to do it. I had a kind of security that I obviously lost upon seeing other films and now I am much more ill at ease in preparing a film" (Ledoux 59–60). If Varda had lost the newcomer's freedom and naïveté by the time she made her second feature, she had nevertheless gained experience, a network of fellow filmmakers, and, notably, an engaged and educated art house audience. This section will focus on the rich film culture that existed in early 1960s Paris, a culture Varda learned to mobilize after making her first feature and that forcefully shaped the fortunes of *Cleo from 5 to 7*.

Cleo chronicles the movements through Paris of a beautiful, initially self-absorbed pop singer who anxiously awaits the results of a medical test that will reveal whether or not she has cancer. The film's title, while evoking the traditional hour for extramarital trysts, implies that we will accompany Cleo from 5:00 to 7:00 PM, and indeed Varda uses many strategies to emphasize duration: the apparent elimination of ellipsis, the multiple shots of clocks, the lengthy journeys by taxi, car, and bus, and the long strolls through a park and the grounds of a hospital. The film's logic is generally casual rather than wholly episodic; Cleo's movements are narratively or spatially justified. She walks from the fortune teller's apartment to a nearby café to meet her assistant; in another café, she hears someone mention her friend Dorothée's name and then decides to pay Dorothée a visit; Dorothée mentions that she needs to pick up a film reel at the train station and so the two of them drive to the Gare Montparnasse. But the film has an episodic quality as well that relies upon coincidence and that moves it away from the classical narrative. Many incidents in *Cléo from 5 to 7* would have been shortened or even elided by a more classical film, such as the scene in which Cleo dreamily tries on hat after hat while the horses of the Republican Guard pass by in the street. Later, by chance, Cleo comes upon a street performer whose act entails swallowing, then disgorging, live frogs. The street performer disgusts and fascinates her but has no obvious narrative function. Instead, the performance suggests obliquely the beginning of Cleo's shift in attention from herself to others and, perhaps, her growing association of the human body with abnormality, illness, or surgery. Most strikingly, her encounter with a soldier (Antoine Bourseiller) on leave from Algeria is generated by sheer coincidence. Upon leaving Dorothée, Cleo wanders in the park and strikes up a conversation with a soldier who accompanies her to the hospital to learn her diagnosis. The overall effect of the narrative construction creates the impression of Cleo wandering from one visually and culturally distinctive place to the next, feeling anxious about her health and looking for answers, distraction, and comfort among friends and strangers alike. This is very far indeed from the goal-driven classical plot.

The film's picaresque narrative reveals both the light causality and the episodic nature of Cleo's afternoon. After having her fortune read, she exits the voyante's apartment and stares at her image in a mirror, noting with obvious pleasure, via internal sound and her expression, that she retains her beauty despite her potential illness. After having coffee with her assistant, Angèle, and purchasing a hat, Cleo takes a lengthy taxi ride through the traffic-ridden Latin Quarter to her apartment in the 14th arrondissement. She exercises briefly and then chats with her lover, a much older, solicitous man. Next she rehearses songs with her lyricist, portrayed by the composer Michel Legrand, but is then overcome with emotion while singing a song about death. She abandons the rehearsal and stomps out of her apartment, frustrated at not being taken seriously by the musicians. While walking to a nearby café, she encounters the frog-swallowing busker. At the café, she plays one of her own songs on the jukebox and strolls around the café listening to people talk. She exits the café, walks down the sidewalk, and appears to contemplate the various people with whom she has been in contact that day. She sees another street performer, then visits her friend, Dorothée, who poses nude for artists. She accompanies Dorothée to the train station to pick up the film reels and then to the cinema where Dorothée's boyfriend works as a projectionist. They watch a comic short film from the projection booth (featuring New Wave compatriots Jean-Luc Godard and Anna Karina) and then take a taxi to the Parc Montsouris, where Dorothée goes her own way as Cleo continues her seemingly aimless stroll. A chatty, friendly soldier on leave from the Algerian war strikes up an acquaintance with Cleo and then accompanies her to the hospital, where she learns that she does indeed have cancer and must get treatment. The ending is ambiguous; it remains unclear whether Cleo is likely to survive, yet she is no longer afraid.

In terms of style, the film foregrounds spatial and temporal continuity and psychological realism, emphasizing both the geography of the 14th arrondissement, Varda's own neighborhood, and Cleo's shifting emotional state as she moves from fear to anger to serenity. Cleo travels from point A to point B over the course of the film's ninety minutes, from the fortune teller's to the hospital, during the hours from 5 to 7 PM. How she gets there and how she passes the time form the substance of *Cleo's* story, providing our only clues to Cleo's state of mind. More significantly, especially for feminist readings, the film shifts from how Cleo looks (i.e., what *we* see) to a subtle but pronounced emphasis on what *she* sees. The film is also an exemplary instance of European art cinema as defined by David Bordwell, with its refreshment of the codes of realism, authorial flourishes such as jump cuts and long takes, and its ambiguous ending. Also in line with European art cinema, Varda uses techniques such as location shooting and the creation of "dead time," choices associated with Italian Neorealism and celebrated by André Bazin. Varda combines her commitment to spatial and temporal realism with several of the visual flourishes Bordwell inventoried, including jump cuts (when Cleo descends the fortune teller's staircase), long takes (in the taxi and the art studio), and mobile framing (in the hat store and the rehearsal scenes). Cleo's subjectivity is emphasized through the soundtrack, both in the first café scene in which her attention shifts from her assistant's nonstop prattle to the couple's dispute at the neighboring table. During the second café scene, Cleo's aural perception and her isolation are again emphasized when she monitors the conversations of those around her, their individual voices rising above the din to comment upon art, literature, and their relationships. Later still, when Cleo walks down the street after exiting the café on her way to find Dorothée, realistic sound drops out altogether and she hears only the tick-tock of a clock while imagining a stylized series of images of friends and café patrons. Such strategies were noticed and appreciated at the time by French critics, who lauded the film for its psychological and documentary realism, its rigorous treatment of temporality, and its fresh way of representing the city of Paris.

Georges Charensol called *Cleo from 5 to 7* a "true modern film, profoundly of our era" and saw it as a kind of snapshot of the year 1961: "Ninety minutes in the life of a Parisian woman can contain the anguish and the preoccupations of a nation" ("Le Coeur révélateur"). Pierre Billard praised the film's "psychological depth," its combination of realism and stylization, and its lack of an obvious "message." Jean-Louis Bory celebrated the film's emphasis on duration, its "chronological rigor," and its "subjective time." For Claude Beylie, "*Cleo* is (among other things) the most beautiful film ever shot in and about Paris." Roger Tailleur wrote, "*Cleo* is . . . both the freest of films and the film that is the greater prisoner of constraints, the most natural and the most formal, the most realistic and the most precious, the most moving to see and the most pleasant to watch." The film would eventually enjoy significant domestic and international success. It attracted a respectable 559,012 viewers in France upon its initial release in 1962 (Simsi 152) and was selected for competition at the Cannes Film Festival. The film was also selected for the "Information Section" of the Venice Film Festival, which runs parallel to the main competition and is designed to inform the public of new impulses in world cinema (Bastide, "Genèse," 312). The film did not win prizes at Cannes or Venice, but it won the Prix Méliès in 1962, an award given by the Syndicat Français de la Critique de Cinéma, the French film critic union, for the best French film or French coproduction (Bastide, "Genèse," 314).

Two novelizations of *Cleo from 5 to 7* were published in 1962; Varda participated in the preparation of both of them. In August 1962 a publisher called Festival Films published a photo-novelization of *Cleo from 5 to 7* aimed at the mass market. The forty-eight-page text combined dialogue from the film, plot description, and 265 production stills taken by Liliane de Kermadec, the photographer hired by the production company Rome Paris Films (Bastide, Diss, 272).

Cleo was the first New Wave film to be chosen by Festival Films for such a treatment. Then in September 1962, the prestigious publisher Éditions Gallimard published a screenplay of the film that included dialogue, plot information, shot scale, and camera movement Since the

One of two novelizations published
after the release of *Cleo from 5 to 7* (1962).
© Ciné-Tamaris

1920s, Gallimard had published a great deal of material on cinema, both theoretical texts as well as film novelizations. As Bastide notes, Gallimard had already published the screenplay for *Hiroshima mon amour*, written by *nouveau roman* proponent Marguerite Duras, but the publication of a Gallimard edition of *Cleo from 5 to 7* was unusual given that Varda was the first person without ties to the literary world to have her script published in this prestigious collection ("Genèse," 284).

Such glowing praise for a film that departed from classical French cinema can be explained in part by the immediate context of the French New Wave, which had defined itself in opposition to mainstream cinema, but also by the unusually effervescent film culture in France that had developed during the twenty years following World War II. Neupert writes of a new journalistic environment that valued both high and low culture and supported the growth of film criticism (Neupert 13). De Baecque highlights the strong and varied intellectual commitments of critics such as André Bazin, Georges Sadoul, Roger Tailleur, and François Truffaut, who engaged in lively disputes over French "quality" cinema, neorealism, and Hollywood cinema in the pages of *Cahiers du cinéma, Revue du cinéma, Positif,* and many other journals throughout the 1950s and beyond (de Baecque, *La cinéphilie*). One result of this critical fermentation was the creation of an environment in which filmmakers felt called upon to experiment, knowing that an alert and sophisticated audience existed for their work. Burnett characterizes this period as one in which "risky" narrative cinema was encouraged because there was a "cultural market for auteur cinema" that promoted a cluster of "social dynamics" between the auteur and the cinephile. These "direct and indirect forms of contact, cooperation and address" proved to auteurs that their works could fruitfully "engage specific communities of supporters, their discourses and their practices" (Burnett).

While de Baecque focuses on the interventions of individual critics in 1950s French film culture and Burnett excavates the specific "feedback loop" between Robert Bresson and his critical community, my focus in this section is on *ciné-clubs*, more and less formal film societies through which people came together to watch and discuss films. One such club, the Ciné-club des Avant-Premières, chose *Cleo* for its inaugural screening and—fortunately for us—left concrete evidence of the richness of the French cultural marketplace for cinema in the form of a postscreening audience questionnaire now held in Ciné-Tamaris's archive. Before examining that rich treasure trove, however, it will be helpful to outline the history and structure of these French film societies.

The *ciné-club* was central to French film culture starting in the immediate postwar period. André Bazin, François Truffaut, and Henri Langlois, founder of the Cinémathèque française in the mid-1930s, were all active in the leadership of *ciné-clubs*, but so were thousands of ordinary viewers all over France. Fifteen years of intensive *ciné-club* activity undoubtedly played a role in the formation of what Alain Resnais identified in 1962 as a "new wave of spectators." When asked about the causes and the consequences of the French New Wave, Resnais responded, "It is less a new wave of directors of which we should speak and more a new wave of spectators. The film culture of the public is infinitely more elevated than it was ten years ago. The young generation of spectators has less prejudice and is more demanding than before. If there really exists a renewal in the current French cinema, we owe it, in large part, to this young generation of spectators" (Chevalier 248). The critical success and broader cultural visibility of *Cleo* is due in part to the *ciné-club* and to Varda's understanding of the need to cultivate viewers for her films.

Ciné-clubs had already played a key role in French film culture in the 1920s, when, as historian Richard Abel notes, they helped elevate film to the status of art, encouraged an awareness of film history through their organization of retrospectives and lectures, and promoted avant-garde, censored, and other noncommercial films (251–57). In the 1930s, after the coming of sound put a damper on the production of avant-garde film, the *ciné-club* became a kind of sanctuary for the silent classics (Jeander 385). During the Occupation, *ciné-clubs* were banned, but they experienced a renaissance in the immediate postwar period. As early as March 1945, the Fédération française des ciné-clubs (FFCC) re-emerged with six clubs, and within one year eighty-three clubs were in operation, with more than fifty thousand members (Pinel 36). By 1962, the year *Cleo* was released, there were approximately five hundred clubs in metropolitan France alone, with an estimated membership of two hundred thousand. The number of films shown is startling: in 1961 alone, approximately six thousand feature films and ten thousand short films were screened in French *ciné-clubs* ("La FFCC à la rue").

Just as notable as the quantitative rejuvenation of the French *ciné-club* in the postwar era is the shift in its goals. The recast postwar *ciné-club* showed a broader range of films and attracted members from a wider socioeconomic spectrum of viewers than had its 1920s predecessors. The goals of the postwar *ciné-club* were succinctly laid out in the title of an article written by film critic and director Pierre Kast in 1945: "Develop Film Taste, Introduce Masterpieces, Educate the Public: That Is the Task of *Ciné-clubs*" (46). The goal of the revived *ciné-club* movement is "to form spectators both fully aware and passionate who will continue to frequent commercial cinemas, more often, if possible, but with another regard and a refined sensibility, more lucid and more acute" (Pinel 41). The *ciné-club* attempted to cultivate "refined" sensibilities in specific ways: through its diverse programming, through film education workshops, and, above all, through *le débat*, the discussion that took place following the screening.

Ciné-club programming in the postwar era was quite diverse. It favored certain directors and national cinemas, certainly, but it included both documentary and fiction films, shorts and features, experimental and genre films, and French and foreign titles. Not surprisingly, films by established *auteurs*, such as Orson Welles, Sergei Eisenstein, Carl Theodor Dreyer, Ingmar Bergman, Luis Buñuel, Jean Cocteau, and Satyajit Ray, were a mainstay of the *ciné-club*. The clubs' programmers also showed a preference for Italian Neorealism, American genre films, French avant-garde short films, and short documentaries. Far from serving as a tool of a French national cinema alone, as one might expect, the *ciné-club* actively promoted films from a variety of countries, including the United States, Italy, Germany, Denmark, India, Russia, and Japan.

Careful programming went hand in hand with the purposeful presentation of the film at the *ciné-club* screenings. For the task of introducing the film to *ciné-club* members and instigating a lively discussion about it, *ciné-clubs* had trained *animateurs* (facilitators). Film history's most famous *animateur* was André Bazin. In the latter half of the 1940s, Bazin was not only publishing his hugely influential articles on Italian Neorealism, Orson Welles, and William Wyler, but he was also making the rounds of schools, factories, union meetings, and *ciné-clubs*, facilitating discussions of films such as Carné's *Le Jour se lève* and Renoir's *Le Crime de M. Lange* (1936) (de Baecque, *La Cinéphilie*, 33–36). The typical *animateur*, however, especially in the provinces, was more likely to be a local schoolteacher with a passion for cinema. Directors of *ciné-clubs* had at their disposal in the early 1960s several primers on how to create a successful *débat*. One such primer was written by Max Egly, a specialist in adult education. Egly advises the *animateur* to begin by soliciting club members' first impressions of the film, then move toward isolating its narrative elements and situating it in its historical framework (256). He warns that viewers should take special care to avoid the reduction of a film to its subject matter alone (261). The viewers should also be encouraged to discuss the film's relationship to the director's biography and oeuvre and, finally, its connections to related films, literature, and other art forms. Egly's essay was published in a book called *Regards neufs sur le cinéma* (*New Perspectives on the Cinema*), part of a series of works devoted to topics such as photography, sport, literature, and the French song. The series was a joint venture of the publisher Editions du Seuil and the organization "Peuple et Culture" (People and Culture), which emerged near the end of the Occupation and was developed by resistance figures contemplating the shape of postwar French culture. The basic goal of Peuple et Culture was to strengthen French culture by building a culture common to all people and specifically to "elevate the cultural level of those from all social milieus, particularly the working class" ("Peuple et culture" 314). Supported by France's Ministry of National Education, Peuple et Culture trained people through courses, workshops, and publications to "animate" cultural organizations such as *ciné-clubs*, book clubs, or music appreciation groups. The *ciné-club*, then, was part of an extensive, well-organized postwar initiative aimed at democratizing culture.

The goals of the postwar *ciné-club* were consequently myriad and ambitious: to reach out to viewers from a wide socioeconomic spectrum, expose them to a range of worthy films from a variety of national traditions, genres, and *auteurs*, and teach them to formulate and express publicly their opinions about the films' narrative, style, and historical context. The *ciné-club* did not aspire to replace the commercial cinema in its members' lives or to promote a renaissance in experimental filmmaking, as had the 1920s *ciné-clubs*. Instead, the postwar *ciné-club* invested in the formation of an active, educated viewer who was not necessarily a writer or an artist. The traces left by the premier of *Cleo from 5 to 7* at the Ciné-club des

Avant-Premières provide evidence that the *ciné-clubs* achieved that goal and also that Varda understood the importance of the clubs in promoting films that departed from the norm. The Club des Avant-Premières was founded in 1962 in Paris by film critic Jean-Louis Bory and André Parinaud, director and editor of *Arts*, respectively. *Arts* was a respected weekly arts and culture magazine for which both Truffaut and Godard wrote in the 1950s and which would play an important role in *Cleo's* launch by drawing attention to the club's activities. The Club des Avant-Premières was founded with the idea of showing sneak previews of new films to its members several days or weeks before the films' general release. In contrast to other *ciné-clubs*, which tended to focus on repertory programming, the Club des Avant-Premières wanted to encourage viewers to see certain films "at the very instant when the film is beginning its career." In the initial announcement of the club's launch, Bory clarified its goal of supporting new films as well as its conception of the *ciné-club* audience: "[T]hanks to *ciné-clubs*, specialized journals, the Cinémathèque and certain Parisian cinemas, there [is an] audience that respects the cinema, considers it a major art and recognizes its right to freedom, to boldness. An audience that accepts a 'difficult,' I mean, 'unusual,' cinema. Our dream is to facilitate the relationship between this cinema and that audience. Establish contact" ("Pourquoi").

The club's initial selection committee consisted of Bory and Parinaud as well as Jean Le Duc, director of programing at Radio-Luxembourg, film critics Pierre Marcabru and Roger Boussinot, novelist Christiane de Rochefort, and film distributor Sam Siritzky ("Comment adhérer").[5] The club chose *Cleo* for its inaugural sessions not only because its leadership admired the film, but also because it perceived *Cleo* as potentially "disconcerting" due to "its construction, its rhythm and its themes" (Bory, "Pourquoi"). The club wanted to have an impact on the film's reception by the general public: "Here is the perfect example of a film that could have a dazzling career or could just as easily be a terrible flop. In our own small way, we will attempt to assure that *Cleo* is a success rather than a flop" (Bory, "Pourquoi"). Bory and Parinaud also demonstrate a refined sense of Varda's place in French film culture in 1962. Although she had only one feature and three short documentaries to her credit, they see her as an important filmmaker of the contemporary moment and as a filmmaker invested in cinematic specificity: "Agnès Varda finds herself today at the head of an oeuvre that some would consider thin, but that we consider important. For Agnès Varda, the cinema is something other than the systematic exploitation of novelistic fiction: the cinema gives us things, beings and problems to see that really exist and that exist today. And in showing these things, Agnès Varda works to find forms of expression that are associated exclusively with the means of expression particular to cinema" ("Pourquoi").

The film was screened three times for club members on April 2 and 3 in three different cinemas scattered around Paris: the Studio Publicis on the Champs-Elysées, the Vendôme (Opéra), and the Gaumont (rue de Grenelle). Six other cities in France were also chosen to show *Cleo* as part of the Ciné-club des Avant-Premières's inaugural venture: Nancy, Bordeaux, Marseille, Lyon, and Nice ("Deuxième spectacle"). In Paris, more than two thousand viewers joined the Club des Avant-Premières and attended one of the three screenings. The traditional *ciné-club* format was used, which included an introduction, a projection, and a discussion.

But the Ciné-club des Avant-Premières also used a tool that was not typical in France: a questionnaire designed to assess viewers' understanding of, appreciation for, and objections to *Cleo from 5 to 7*. The questionnaire consisted of eight questions written by Varda herself:

(1) Did you like this film? Why? If you didn't like it, also say why.
(2) Were you more responsive to
    ° the subject?
    ° the directing?
    ° the characters?
(3) What moment (or scene) of the film is your favorite?
(4) Did the film seem to have slow moments? When? Conversely, does the film lack a scene (or a line or an image) that would have provided for better comprehension of the storyline or the characters?
(5) In your opinion, will the young woman, Cléo, die?
(6) What do you think of the roles played by the male characters in this story?
(7) Do you see a greater meaning in this film that goes beyond the storyline itself?
(8) Will you recommend this film to your friends and family?

More than a thousand viewers returned the questionnaire to the offices of *Arts* within the required eight-day period. *Arts* tabulated the responses and reported the results in its April 18–24 issue. The questionnaires were then sent to Agnès Varda, who read and retained a selection of them (eighty-six, to be precise) in the company's records.

These questionnaires serve as a glimpse at the response to a film perceived as worthy, but potentially "difficult." On the whole, the viewers provided detailed and sophisticated responses, analyzing both the film's style and narrative and often placing the film in the contexts of the New Wave and international film history. The questionnaires provide valuable information about art cinema spectatorship during the French New Wave and suggest that Resnais was correct in asserting that a "new wave of spectators" had emerged.

Immediately notable is the diversity of the respondents' professions, especially compared to the 1920s *ciné-club* gatherings, which tended to attract writers and artists. While a significant number of the respondents were, predictably, university students (27 out of 86) or educators (6 out of 86), a wide range of occupations is represented. Respondents included five secretaries, three doctors, two assistant film directors, two accountants, two administrators, two pharmacists, two artists, two journalists, two civil servants, two shopkeepers and one each of the following: librarian, publisher, bank employee, insurance inspector, silk painter, restaurateur, psychologist, engineer, nurse, dry cleaner, interior decorator, writer of radio plays, architect, editor, and translator. One respondent identified herself as a "college graduate in English." Twelve respondents did not have a profession or chose not to divulge it. Three respondents listed "cinéphile" as their profession. Some of the respondents later became important members of the film community. Serge Daney, who would become an influential film critic in the 1970s and 1980s, filled out a questionnaire, as did Roger Diamantis, then a restaurateur who later became an important art house exhibitor with the cinema St. André des Arts.[6] If the socioeconomic makeup of this particular club did not fully reflect the utopian goal of Peuple et Culture to bring the arts to the proletariat, it hints, at least, at the existence of a diverse audience for unconventional films.

The general response to *Cleo* was positive. Many respondents filled out the questionnaire and then added several pages to it, sometimes

CINE-CLUB   A 4

des

AVANT - PREMIERES

140 rue du Fg St-Honoré
    PARIS 8°

                          QUESTIONNAIRE   Prière de nous adresser
                              sur   votre réponse dans les
                                                           8 jours suivant la pro-
                       " C L E O   DE   5   A   7 "   jection et

Nom : DANEY   votre r é p o n s e sera
Prénom : Serge   d'Agnès Varda   transmise au
Adresse : 14 rue des Tallandiers
Ville : Paris   metteur en scène
Profession : étudiant, mais surtout Cinéphile

1/ Avez-vous aimé ce film ?   BEAUCOUP

   Pourquoi ?
   ~~Le beauté~~ L'intelligence, le finesse, l'acuité, l'humour du regard qu'Agnès Varda pose sur
   le monde, transmue toute chose et la rend belle, étrange, inquiétante
   ce film est la continuation... abonissement de tout un cinéma dit "Littéraire" qui passe par Resnais et
   Si vous ne l'avez pas aimé, dites aussi pourquoi,   Cayrol... mais ici je crois que
   l'élément Littéraire disparaît
   (malgré quelques provocations comme
   le découpage en chapitres) et débouche sur
   une beauté purement cinématographique

2/ Avez-vous été davantage sensible :

   - au sujet ?   SECONDAIRE, n'est qu'un prétexte à une mise-en-scène....
   - à la réalisation ?   MERVEILLEUSE, pleine d'inventions... photo très belle.
   - aux personnages ?   CORINNE MARCHAND ; EXTRAORDINAIRE le film vaut d'être vu rien
                                                que pour elle

3/ Quel moment (ou scène) du film préférez-vous ?
   LA REPETITION DES CHANSONS CHEZ CORINNE.
   DOROTHEE BLANK VUE PAR LA VITRE D'UN TAXI, MONTANT DES ESCALIERS.
   SCENE DU PARC MONTSOURIS.
4/ Le film vous a-t-il paru comporter des longueurs ? A quel moment ?
                           NON
   Inversement, manque-t-il une scène (ou une réplique, ou une image) pour
   une meilleure compréhension de l'anecdote ou des personnages ?
   Il faut juger ce qui est sur l'écran et qui forme un tout et non pas ce qu'on aurait voulu y voir.

5/ A votre avis, cette jeune femme, Cléo, est-elle condamnée ?
   AUCUNE IMPORTANCE — ce qui compte c'est le regard qu'on jour sur le monde lorsqu'on se croit condamné
6/ Que pensez-vous du rôle que jouent les personnages masculins dans cette
   histoire ?
   Chacun reflète un aspect de la vie de Cléo. L'amant correspond à tout ce qu'il y a de mondain, de
   frivole (scène de la modiste) chez Cléo, le pianiste correspond au métier d'elle, à son art et enfin
   Antoine est une sorte de découverte par Cléo d'un aspect inconnu d'elle-même : un amour simple et profond
   qu'elle croyait n'avoir jamais connu jusque-là [fin du film]. Cléo grâce à lui, se découvre elle-même
7/ Voyez-vous à ce film une signification qui dépasse l'anecdote elle-même ?
   ce morceau pourrait-être une phrase de Sénèque : "il faut vivre comme si l'on devait mourir le lendemain"
   Ainsi chaque chose prend une valeur, un relief nouveau et jamais la débauche sur une sorte de
   Eurydice et un amour.
8/ Encouragerez-vous votre entourage, vos amis, à aller voir ce film ?
                  Absolument

in the form of a written or typed letter to Varda. Some respondents answered each and every question, while others left some questions unanswered or dispensed with the questionnaire altogether and simply wrote a long analysis of the film. Viewers expressed a surprising familiarity with Varda and her work. Several asked to meet with her, and one viewer even invited her to dinner. Specific scenes frequently singled out for praise in the questionnaires include the hat shop episode, the long taxi ride through Paris, Cleo's rehearsal with her composers, the silent film within the film, and the encounter between Cleo and Antoine near the end. When asked whether they were more sensitive to the film's subject, direction, or characters, viewers frequently refused to separate these elements and instead expressed appreciation for each category or for the film as a whole. Here we can assume that the respondents had successfully absorbed the warning in the *ciné-club* primers about reducing a film to its subject matter or to its themes alone. Likewise, respondents tended not to object to the plot's relatively open ending. Most respondents believed Cleo has a terminal illness but viewed the process of her transformation throughout the film as more important than her specific prognosis.

In keeping with the advice given in the *ciné-club* primers, the viewers of *Cleo* tended to comment at length on both narrative and film style. One student from Paris commented on the contrast between color and black-and-white stock at the beginning of the film, the play of mirrors and windows in the hat shop scene, and the shift in the background from white to black when Cleo begins to sing her song. Another viewer, a law student from Bordeaux, established links between style and narrative. "The film's technique is very adapted to the characters and especially to the spirit of the author: the excellent camera movements around the piano with the bizarre musicians . . . the very good scenes in the interior of the hat shop where the apparent disorganization of the camera only shows Cleo's disarray."

Some caution is prudent in assessing the extent to which viewers felt positively about *Cleo*. Because of its affiliation with Club des Avant-Premières, *Arts* had an interest in the success of the film. Moreover, it is possible that the people who filled out the questionnaires knew that Agnès Varda would likely be reading their responses, so perhaps some viewers expressed an inflated degree of enthusiasm for the film. Yet not all the respondents provided positive and lengthy comments on the film. Many were content to fill out the form in a cursory fashion, and a few were quite critical of the film. One particularly disgruntled viewer, who identified herself as a "bilingual stenographer," wrote that the film was "idiotic" and that she wanted to be reimbursed. Another viewer, a university student in Paris, was "bored" by the film, finding Cleo "egotistical" and the soldier "ugly" and "without charm." Yet, surprisingly, even viewers who disliked *Cleo* provide subtle comments about the film's style, discussing individual scenes and shots in detail. For example, one viewer who objected to many things in the film observed, "The film is a kind of photographic reportage with sound, a *cinéma-vérité* on a star, in the streets of Paris. . . . in a hat store, the singing star's 'studio,' and a sculpture studio. It is a visual magazine, a kind of filmic *Elle* or *Marie France* that one flips through, [seeing] a model trying on hats [and] a female taxi driver recounting an attack."

Here it is as if the viewer is heeding the advice of *animateur* Max Egly to find connections between films and other kinds of texts: *cinéma vérité* documentary, photojournalism, and women's magazines. This viewer even suggests that the film's style invites a particular viewing mode: one "flips through" the film. Surprisingly, the viewer's denigration of *Cleo from 5 to 7*—he links it, after all, to a lowbrow cultural object, the woman's magazine—coexists with his admiration of the film's settings and cinematography. Cleo's strolls through Paris, he notes, evoke those of Jeanne Moreau in Louis Malle's *Ascenseur pour l'échafaud* (*Elevator to the Gallows*, 1958), and the film's cinematography is "remarkable." Another viewer compares *Cleo* unfavorably to Truffaut's *Jules et Jim* (*Jules and Jim*, 1962), but comments on Varda's use of color stock in the film's prologue and on specific edits. He complains that the scene in the hat shop is "too much like a romance novel" and even speculates that the peignoir worn by Cleo was previously used in Resnais's *L'Année dernière à Marienbad* (*Last Year at Marienbad*, 1961). This viewer disliked *Cleo from 5 to 7*, yet he takes the film seriously enough to watch it carefully and to dissect its visual style.

The *ciné-club* members' ability to discuss both style and narrative is notable, but equally remarkable is their ability to place the film in the context of film history. Sometimes this comparative activity works in a negative sense. Viewers specify what the film *is* by saying what it is *not*.

For example, a university student from Paris distinguished *Cleo* from Hollywood cinema, noting the film's lack of a concluding kiss:

> Everyone was waiting . . . with a sort of conditioned reflex, for a kiss, like in all American films, which resemble each other. . . . and then, no. Three little notes and it was over! Ha! If you had seen the theater, in which we behaved exactly like Pavlov's dog. [It was as if one had] conducted an experiment on conditioned reflex. . . . The audience let out a little cry as if it was disappointed that one had not flattered and exploited its sexual urges!! This was good; you brought us out of our routine.

A student from Valence distinguished *Cleo* from "traditional cinema" for its relative de-dramatization: "The film pulls the spectator out of his comfort. If someone asked us what we just saw, we would easily respond: nothing. There is no dramatic event, no theatrical coup. . . . We are offered insignificant, unoriginal, unlinked facts. And yet we are moved, touched, troubled."

Others linked *Cleo* in a positive manner to specific films. To the question "Would you encourage your friends to see this film?" a medical student replied, "That depends. To love this film, it is necessary, I believe, to have loved *Pickpocket* [Bresson, 1959], for example, and perhaps also *Lola* [Demy, 1961]." The student from Valence revealed her familiarity with other eras and traditions of filmmaking in her response to the same question. "As for me, I know that I can place *Cleo from 5 to 7* in my imaginary *cinémathèque* next to *Night and Fog* and *A Day in the Country*." A law student living in Bordeaux wrote that the tracking shots in the hospital garden reminded him of the tracking shots in Resnais's *Hiroshima mon amour* and that the character of Cleo recalled Lola in Demy's film. The depth of field used in Cleo's apartment reminded him of *Citizen Kane*, no less. Another viewer disliked the film's visual style, but argued that Cleo is a new kind of heroine with links to other New Wave female protagonists: "This is a delicious painting of a woman. Corinne Marchand is, I believe, the most 'true' of the modern heroines. These last months have been full of them! Bardot in *Vie privée*, Moreau in *Jules et Jim*, Karina in *Une femme est une femme* and not long ago, Anouk Aimée in *Lola*. Cleo adds a character to the New Wave's gallery of 'modern heroines.'"

Viewers also placed the film in the context of Varda's own work, citing her first feature, *La Pointe Courte*, and the three short films she made in the late 1950s. One viewer observed that Varda's *L'Opéra-Mouffe* helped him understand *Cleo from 5 to 7*, since both allow us to "enter into the psychological world of [a] woman." Viewers were thus able to place *Cleo* in several contexts: Varda's oeuvre, the French New Wave, and film history more generally.

The questionnaires on *Cleo* in the Club des Avant-Premières suggest that the pedagogical goals of the *ciné-club* had indeed been achieved. First, the club chose to celebrate the work of a marginalized filmmaker whose works were understood as "difficult" and thus adhered to the long-standing *ciné-club* tradition of exposing viewers to unconventional films. The respondents write of Varda as an *auteur*, linking *Cleo* to her earlier films and characterizing Varda's thematic and stylistic preoccupations. Not only do the viewers possess a context for Varda's films, they have a broader understanding of film history, reflected in references to Antonioni, Renoir, and Welles. Above all, the respondents are sensitive to film narrative and style; they write of the overall arc of the film's narrative and its unconventional conclusion and provide detailed commentary on lighting, camera movement, and set design. The *Cleo* questionnaires thus suggest the existence of a cultivated and confident art house spectator keenly attuned to matters of film form, style, and narrative.

The questionnaires are also interesting for what they reveal about Varda's conception of her viewers. It was not common practice to organize test screenings of films in 1960s France, so Varda stands out for her desire to test the effect of her film on the spectators. The questionnaires confirmed for Varda that viewers could tolerate ambiguity. "I understood that one should never underestimate the intelligence and comprehension of the audience, despite what professional distributors and the purveyors of big spectacles say" (Varda, interview with the author, 2003). In her subsequent filmmaking practice, Varda would continue to solicit her viewers' opinions in both formal and informal ways.

Thanks to the insight provided by these questionnaires, a more detailed profile of the "demanding" viewer intuited by Alain Resnais in 1962 now emerges. Spectators nurtured in the context of post–World War II efforts at cultural democratization likely believed they had a right to access the arts, to experience all kinds of cinema, music, theater, and literature, no matter their socioeconomic origins. Such viewers tended not to make a living in the arts or have links to the film industry but nevertheless wanted to view and discuss films on a regular basis. Such spectators understood that noncommercial cinema required the support of viewers and perceived themselves as actors in the cultural scene, capable of shifting the fortunes of individual films and of having an impact on the broader film culture. *Ciné-club* viewers had a nuanced understanding of the New Wave and some understanding of world film history, were open to new storytelling strategies, had developed a vocabulary for describing film style, and were sensitive to the relationship between film style and narrative.

The *ciné-club* played a central role in supporting Varda's work, but no less important was the role of the press. In addition to helping launch the Ciné-club des Premières, *Arts* further supported *Cleo* by publishing positive reviews of the film in its April 18–24 issue. Bory's review, titled "Cleo from 5 to 7 Is a Masterpiece," dubbed Varda "the Virginia Woolf of modern cinema" due to the film's "extremely rigorous chronological frame" evocative of that of *Mrs. Dalloway* (Bory, "Cléo"). In that same issue was an article reporting on the questionnaire, which asserted that 97 percent of the respondents liked the film and that the club would now expand to the provinces.[7] In the May 9–15 issue of *Arts*, it was reported that the film was enjoying a positive reception in the provinces. The club went so far as to claim responsibility for the film's success: "The demonstration that we just made in Paris and that we are pursuing in the provinces, with *Cleo*, proves it. Unusual film, a film *hors série*, an *auteur* film, a difficult film in the context of traditional exhibition, *Cleo from 5 to 7* found its audience thanks to the Club" ("Le Club"). In the May 16–22 issue of *Arts*, it was reported that the film received an excellent reception in Marseille and Bordeaux and that it would soon be shown in *ciné-club*s in Grenoble, Lyon, Strasbourg, Nevers, Tours, Clermont-Ferrand, Saint-Etienne, and Pau ("Cléo a conquis"). In that same issue, Pierre Marcabru, member of the selection committee of Ciné-club des Avant-Premières, reported as a special envoy to the Cannes Film Festival that *Cleo* was the "only truly original film" showing at the festival. Finally, in the June 20–26 issue of *Arts*, Bory published an essay titled "What Has Changed in Cinema in the Last Ten Years," in which he discusses all the ways in which *Cleo* was the epitome of the "modern" film.[8]

Arts was not the only publication to contribute to the launch of *Cleo from 5 to 7*. As Bastide points out in his astute analysis of the *Cleo* launch, many journalists visited the set of the film and reported on the production ("Genèse"). As early as August 1961, articles about the production of *Cleo* began appearing in publications such as *Le Figaro littéraire*, *Télérama*, *L'Express*, and *Heures claires* (Bastide, "Genèse," 234). Over a period of eighteen months, between April 1961 and winter 1962, seven different publicity inserts were purchased and placed in trade publications such as *Cinématographie française* and *Film français* (Bastide, "Genèse," 235). Printed in the film's marketing material were brief, adulatory phrases from celebrities including Alain Resnais, Jacques Prévert, Michelangelo Antonioni, André Cayatte (then president of the "Commission of Quality" at the Centre National de la Cinématographie and member of the selection committee of the Cannes Film Festival), Michèle Morgan, Monica Vitti, Annie Girardot, Brigitte Bardot, and Françoise Sagan (Bastide, "Genèse," 243).

Upon the film's initial release, Varda contributed directly to the enthusiastic reception of the film and its interpretation by giving more than twenty lengthy interviews to the French press alone and many more to regional and international publications. Varda contributed to the creation of positive word of mouth about the film among the Paris intelligentsia in other ways, as well. Her notebooks from late October and early November 1961 reveal that she created lists of guests to be invited to the press screenings of the film. On the list, as expected, were the important film critics of the day (Georges Charensol, Jean de Baroncelli, Georges Sadoul, among many others) and fellow film directors (Godard, Marker, Rivette, Truffaut, Resnais, Chabrol, Melville, etc.), but also curators and programmers such as Jacques Ledoux and Mary Meerson, and the novelists Nathalie Sarraute and Raymond Queneau.

Other facets of *Cleo's* distribution contributed to its success. The film was distributed by Athos Films, a company active since the 1930s in Paris and headed by Russian émigrés Sam and Jo Siritzky. Athos was known for its support of European art cinema; it premiered Chabrol's *Le Beau Serge* (1958) and Antonioni's *L'Avventura* at the Studio Publicis. Athos's strategy was to place films strategically in first-run, medium-sized cinemas containing only five to six hundred seats (Bastide, "Genèse," 231). The theatrical premier of *Cleo* took place on April 11, 1962, in three cinemas in different neighborhoods of Paris: the Gaumont-Rive Gauche in Montparnasse, the Studio Publicis on the Champs-Elysées, and the Vendôme near the Opera. *Cleo* played for seven weeks in Paris before moving to other cities in France and to Monaco, Corsica, Algeria, Tunisia, and Morocco. The film was seen by 263,911 viewers in Paris, far fewer than the Paris viewership for mainstream films released in France in 1961 and 1962, such as *West Side Story* (seen by 2,492,814) and *The Longest Day*, a Hollywood film about the D-day invasion (seen by 1,611,513 in Paris), but close to the viewership for *Lola* (236,185) and Billy Wilder's *The Apartment* (352,295) (Simsi 27).

The successful launch of *Cleo from 5 to 7* was the result of many cultural forces, including *ciné-club* culture, film criticism, innovative distributors, and fellow filmmakers and actors willing to lend their charisma to an unusual film. Varda understood, in 1962 and throughout the subsequent decades, that films require much more than their inherent qualities to remain visible, even in the culture of art house cinema. The unusual longevity of *Cleo's* visibility in film culture through the decades is due in no small part to Varda's willingness to accompany the film to countless festivals and retrospectives, her skill at speaking intelligently with journalists and scholars about her work, and her ability to attract attention to her film through its successive releases on VHS and DVD.

Improvisation and Formal Patterning: *Vagabond*

Cleo from 5 to 7 brought Varda international recognition and full membership in the French New Wave. Also in 1962, Varda married Demy, who adopted Rosalie, Varda's daughter with *Cleo* actor Antoine Bourseiller. Varda then traveled to Cuba and shot an innovative short documentary called *Salut les Cubains* (1963), made up primarily of still images. Her controversial and brilliant third feature, *Le Bonheur* (*Happiness*, 1965), offered an exquisitely shot, ambiguous portrait of a traditional family, while *Les Créatures* (*The Creatures*, 1966) featured Catherine Deneuve (so emblematic of Demy's work) and Michel Piccoli (with Belmondo and Brialy, the face of the New Wave) in a sci-fi–art film hybrid shot the same year as Godard's *Alphaville*.

Varda and Demy lived in Los Angeles from 1967 to 1969, where Demy made *Model Shop* (1969) for Columbia Pictures and Varda made two shorts and one feature. Varda's happy immersion in the political and popular culture of America in the late 1960s reveals itself in her films' subjects and styles. *Uncle Yanco* (1967) is a portrait of her artist-uncle living on a houseboat in Sausalito, while *Black Panthers* (1968) documents the Black Power movement in Oakland. Varda's feature *Lions Love* (1969) brought together Viva, *Hair* authors James Rado and Gerome Ragni, and experimental filmmaker Shirley Clarke in a largely improvised fiction feature about three actors living in Hollywood.

Back in France, Varda gave birth to Mathieu Demy in 1972. She then released a feature-length documentary about the daily lives of her neighbors, *Daguerréotypes* (1974), and then directed *L'Une chante, l'autre pas* (*One Sings, the Other Doesn't*, 1976), a folk musical about female friendship and the fight for women's rights. Varda and Demy separated for much of the 1980s; he moved across the street from Varda but continued to be present in the lives of their children. In 1980, once again living in Los Angeles, Varda made *Mur Murs* (1980), a feature documentary about street murals followed by a fiction feature titled *Documenteur* (1980–81). *Documenteur* is a poetic, long-take film about a lonely single mother, played by Varda's editor Sabine Mamou, living in Los Angeles with her son, played by Varda's own son, Mathieu Demy. The film remains Varda's personal favorite, offering further elements of fragmented self-portraiture at a time when Varda's prodigious creativity was offset by a painful isolation.

Back in Paris once again, Varda made a reflexive short documentary about a photograph she had made twenty years previously, a meditation on memory entitled *Ulysse* (1982) as well as *Une minute pour une image* (*One Minute for an Image*, 1983), a television series consisting of 170 programs, each lasting two minutes and offering an analysis of one photograph, broadcast nightly over a period of six months. In 1984, Varda made two more short films, *Les Dites cariatides* (*The So-called Caryatids*), a poetic study of architectural statuary in Paris, and *7 P., Cuis., S. de b. . . . (à saisir)* (literally *7 rms, kitch. bath . . . will go fast*), an experimental film.

Then in 1985, Varda made *Sans toit ni loi* (*Vagabond*), her best-known feature, which chronicled the final two months in the life of a young woman wandering in the south of France during a bitterly cold winter. The French title plays on an expression in French, *sans foi ni loi*, "godless and lawless," with its connotation of both fearlessness and ruthlessness, or in the case of Varda's heroine, rooflessness. Given how difficult this would have been to convey in a commercial title in English, the term "vagabond" seems both suggestive and enigmatic enough to evoke similar associations in the minds of Anglophone audiences.

Considered by many to be Varda's most impressive work, this project emerged improbably at a low point in her career. She had returned to France in 1981 following her second sojourn to Los Angeles. Back in Paris, finding funding to shoot another feature was so difficult that she nearly gave up feature-length filmmaking (Varda and Bonnaire). Nevertheless, she forged ahead with the making of *Vagabond*, inspired by her positive experience with the experimental shorts filmed in the summer of 1984. Despite her enthusiasm, nothing about *Vagabond*—the financing, the shoot itself, securing a distributor—would be easy.

The film opens with the discovery of a young woman's corpse in a ditch, flashes back to trace the final weeks in her life, and concludes where the film began, with her body in the ditch. The flashback structure undercuts suspense; from the beginning, we know that Mona dies of exposure.[9] More striking than the fact of Mona's death is the narrative's construction of a complex, ultimately unknowable female protagonist, harking back to the structure and conceit of *Cleo*, albeit it in a darker, grimmer reality without the vibrant Parisian travelogue. The film offers little explanation of Mona's motivations or desires. We learn about her by watching her interact with the people she encounters on the road—a professor who specializes in diseased trees, a garage mechanic, a Moroccan vineyard worker, a maid, a goatherder, and fellow drifters—as well as through eighteen "testimonials," in some cases spoken directly to the camera, some to an off-screen interviewer (Varda) in the style of a news report, and others to another person on-screen in a simple two-shot (Flitterman-Lewis 304). Over time, such testimonials and conversations provide a composite portrait of Mona that nevertheless remains incomplete. The only concrete facts we know about her are that she once worked in an office as a secretary, did not like having a boss, is estranged from her family, and likes pop music and smoking dope. We infer that she prefers solitude and movement to commitment and stasis, but we never know precisely what compelled her to take to the road. With *Vagabond*, Varda added a new element of experimentation: the construction of a complex female character who embodied the ultimate unknowability. Varda's planning notes emphasize the opacity of her protagonist: "we never know what Mona thinks" and "she says very little about herself." It's not that Varda had not bothered to think through Mona's backstory. An early draft of the screenplay contains an exchange between Mona and Professor Landier, the tree plague expert, in which Mona speaks of having lived with foster families and in an orphanage with her three siblings, but even this fragment of information was withheld from the final version of the film (Varda, Ciné-Tamaris Archive, *Sans toit ni loi*). Instead, Varda's goal was to "show the facts and the gestures of Mona, seen, recounted or thought by others." In *Varda par Agnès*, Varda calls her characterization of Mona a "puzzle-portrait" (59). In the many interviews she has given about *Vagabond*, Varda emphasizes that instead of constructing a conventional character, she wanted to capture Mona's gestures and her daily movements. "What interests me is how Mona lives out her days, how she bears the cold and the solitude and why she walks and where" (Varda, *Varda par Agnès*, 59). In many ways, Varda is anticipating the observational gleaning that will form the basis of later films and art installations, and that I personally witnessed in Montreal in 2005.

Contrary to classical film narrative, *Vagabond* does not work to produce a coherent explanation of the forces that drive Mona toward her death or to construct a character with clear goals and motivations. Nor is Varda's goal, particularly, to enhance our empathy for a homeless woman vulnerable to hunger, rape, and exposure. Instead, the film works to render concretely, in a highly patterned fashion, the material daily events that make up Mona's existence. The film's very structure underscores this truncated characterization of Mona. The narrative consists of many relatively brief, fragmented episodes chronicling Mona's life on the road. Many of the scenes involve Mona's encounters with strangers: she asks for water or matches, is awakened in her tent by a cemetery caretaker, eats a bowl of soup offered by a nun, and works petty jobs for cash. Longer scenes chronicle her encounters with a number of people, including David, a fellow drifter who becomes Mona's lover for a few days. Mona is not searching for rescue. Goatherders offer her land for cultivating potatoes but eventually give up on her due to her laziness. The housemaid Yolande befriends Mona, only to reject her upon discovering her drinking and laughing with her employer, Aunt Lydie, a breach in etiquette that is too transgressive of the social order for Yolande's comfort; just who is dependent on whom? The testimonial scenes about Mona create a further rupture in the film's fragmented narrative trajectory. One especially striking scene consists of a shot of Assoun, a sympathetic man who teaches Mona how to work in a vineyard but asks her to leave upon the return of his coworkers. Just before the scene in the village in which revelers will chase Mona, Assoun stares directly into the camera and says nothing. His silence distinguishes him from the other witnesses. His connection to Mona remains unspoken, but his gesture of smelling the red scarf she left behind leaves no doubt about his love for her. Despite the number of such "testimonial" scenes, by the end of the film we are no closer to understanding Mona's rejection of, and by, society. Viewers are not asked to understand, pity, or judge Mona; instead, they are simply invited to watch her move through various landscapes and interact with many people, some of whom envy and admire her for her independence, most of whom do in fact judge her, mitigating our own judgments. As Varda suggests in an interview, "In accompanying Mona, the film suggests everyone's intolerance regarding those who are not within the norm" (Alion 5).

A first viewing of the film might give one the impression that *Vagabond*'s narrative is a string of random episodes, but Varda inventively links scenes together using a multiplicity of techniques. Sometimes the links are both verbal and visual, as in the beginning of the film when we hear Varda in voice-over: "I know little about her myself, but it seems to me she came from the sea." Varda's voice-over is accompanied by the image of Mona emerging from the ocean, nude. The subsequent scene begins with a shot of postcards featuring nude women outside a café, an echo of the nude Mona. Sometimes such links between scenes work to diminish the credibility of a character. For instance, later in the film, the mechanic says to the camera, "Drifters all alike, just flirts and loafers." Yet prior to this, in flashback, we saw Mona working hard in the mechanic's garage washing a car, neither loafing nor chasing men.

The obvious desire with which the mechanic eyes Mona brings a hint of a smile to her face, which promptly fades. She *is* capable of working hard; and *he* is the one who pursued her, the editing implies.

The bulk of the narrative offers scenes featuring Mona alone or with one other person. The scene in the Nîmes train station is different, however, as it brings together most of the characters and narrative threads, something Varda avoided so resolutely at the beginning of her cinematic experimentation with *La Pointe Courte*. Indeed, Varda's early planning notes for *Vagabond* reveal that she initially conceived the film as a kind of network narrative. One of the earliest treatments of the film, which was initially titled *A Saisir*, describes eight characters whose paths cross intermittently (Varda, Ciné-Tamaris Archive, Sans toit ni loi, "A Saisir"). Remnants of this idea remain in the film's final shape. In the scene at the train station toward the end of the film, most of the characters come together. Yolande, who is Aunt Lydie's maid and Paolo's girlfriend, as well as the niece of the caretaker of the chateau and Mona's hostess during her brief stay (she is a veritable network of relations unto herself), arrives at the station to travel to her new job after losing her place with Aunt Lydie in the fallout from Mona's stay. Accompanying Yolande is Jean-Pierre, Aunt Lydie's nephew and the assistant of plane tree specialist Professor Landier (yet another intersecting network of relationships). Yolande sees Mona and, startled, communicates her shock directly to the camera. A drunken Mona, meanwhile, kisses the pimp who hopes to put her to work in pornographic films and so does not see her former lover David enter the train station and accuse another drifter of stealing money from him. Nephew Jean-Pierre, who is seeing off Yolande as a courtesy, also sees Mona and feels impelled to phone a friend to share his revulsion about Mona's public drunkenness. Two other *marginaux* sit on a bench chatting, one an elderly man to whom Mona had earlier tried to fence stolen silver spoons. They trade anecdotes about having grown up in an orphanage. This highly condensed scene, with its crossed trajectories and coincidences, constitutes the apex of Mona's interactions and suggests that all the film's characters are linked in some way, each with their vulnerabilities, each joined also through levels of judgment, despite their individual and interconnected shortcomings.

This scene, however, is followed by two more fragmented episodes that, far from extending this sense of connection between Mona and others, emphasize the random quality of events in her life, and each succeeds in terrifying Mona. Half asleep and perhaps still drunk, she makes a hasty escape from a burning house. Next, she has a confusing encounter with nameless, costumed villagers engaged in an annual bacchanalian celebration in which they aggressively drench people—Mona included—in wine dregs. Mona flees the revelers, loses the sleeping bag she had wrapped around her shoulders, and wanders, cold and disoriented, until she stumbles and falls into a ditch, where she soon dies of exposure. The narrative thus contains a kind of climax of human interaction and causality (one cannot avoid trying to assign some blame in the circumstances that lead to her death) before reinforcing Mona's utter solitude, her isolation from any community, and the episodic, coincidental quality of the film as a whole.

The film's rising tension and violence are emphasized in yet another way: through the interspersing of twelve sequence shots underscored by the haunting music of composer Joanna Bruzdowicz. Recurring every five minutes or so, the shots track Mona laterally as she moves screen left, and then leave her behind, often coming to rest on something inanimate, such as rusted farm machinery or a road sign. Though the twelve shots are unpredictably scattered throughout the film, graphic matches and compositional patterns establish a connection between them. For example, the first tracking shot comes to rest on a road sign, while the second tracking shot begins by framing a different road sign. One tracking shot comes to rest on a phone booth while the subsequent tracking shot begins with an image of a different phone booth. The music becomes increasingly intense, suggesting Mona's intensifying fragility and withdrawal. Flitterman-Lewis correctly asserts that these shots are "moments of critical distancing, textual spaces that provoke the viewer's analytic reflection" (308).

The idea for the series of tracking shots came late in the production process for Varda. Five weeks into the production, after a preliminary edit, Varda felt she had not yet managed to convey the central fact of Mona's nearly incessant walking. She decided to add a series of tracking shots, which she eventually called the "Travellings de la Grande série," (the "great series" tracking shots). These shots, Varda felt, would impart the feeling that walking is the central, defining fact of Mona's life, more fundamental than her interactions with people. The tracking shots would be united by graphic matches and by the use of Bruzdowicz's spare, nondiegetic music. Most of these shots feature Mona walking through an unidentified landscape. Several contribute more directly to the plot, notably the tracking shot that incorporates the off-screen rape of Mona. Varda's decision to include the twelve shots added five days to the shooting schedule, but the shots provide the film's most notable pattern, and they effectively underscore Varda's characterization of a woman on the move through a series of landscapes, unknowable and rebellious. Here we can see a shift in Varda's working methods from earlier in her career. By 1985, Varda had gained enough confidence as a filmmaker to incorporate flexibility and spontaneity on the set. It is interesting to note that this instance of spontaneity provided a formal contrast to the haphazard, improvisational feel of the scenes of Mona's encounters with the characters populating the film, those fragmented moments when her forward march (shown as an afterthought) is halted and the film tries to piece together more parts to the puzzle of Mona's social interactions.

Varda's working method for *Vagabond* also echoes several strategies she used early in her career.[10] She began researching the film in November 1984 and initially planned to make a short "linear" film, made up solely of exteriors and shot in the winter in the south of France. Indeed, she had wanted to make a film that was the opposite of her short, experimental film *7 P., Cuis., S.d.b . . . (à saisir)*, a film that provided glimpses, sometimes quite humorous, of the daily lives of a traditional nuclear family headed by a patriarch and containing a rebellious teenage girl. Included in its cast were Yolande Moreau, anticipating her role as the maid in *Vagabond*, and Marthe Jarnias, who played Aunt Lydie in the second film. Varda's short—one of her most experimental works—was shot in a former rest home, a space that also housed an art exhibition held in the summer of 1984 in connection with the Festival d'Avignon titled "The Living and the Artificial." The exhibition was macabre in tone and mixed the natural and artifical in intriguing ways, allowing Varda at that early stage to explore installation work (albeit not her own). A room representing a kitchen, for example, featured grass growing on the countertops and birds walking around freely. Varda incorporated the bizarre décor from the exhibition to convey a quality of strangeness, even menace, in the family. The experience of improvising this experimental short provoked in Varda an "irresistible" desire to shoot again right away. "I felt it worked well for me to not wait, not to prepare too much" (Ciné-Tamaris Archive, *Sans toit ni loi*). Varda's initial goals, then, with *Vagabond* were to quickly make another film outdoors, capitalizing on the creative energy and renewed confidence she had gained from making the experimental short.

In imagining *Vagabond*, Varda was inspired politically by the news reports about the "new poor" circulating in the press in the mid-1980s (*Varda par Agnès*, 166). She had long been interested in exploring, understanding, and documenting the lives of those who live in poverty or are marginalized in some way. *La Pointe Courte* had documented in considerable detail the daily work routines of fishermen and their wives; *Ô saisons, Ô chateaux* dwelled on the gardeners and the caretakers working at the castles of the Loire Valley; *L'Opéra-Mouffe* touched on the poverty and alcoholism of the inhabitants of rue Mouffetard. In the mid-1980s, Varda was moved anew by the fact that people were still dying of exposure in the modern world. Homing in on the subject matter of *Vagabond*, Varda was told by a policeman from the Gard region that he had come upon a young man frozen to death underneath an apple tree (Denoyan). "I said to myself: in our modern, extraordinary, developed, heated world, there are people on the road or in the ditches who die of cold. That was the first emotion" (Philipe and Pagès). With this initial idea in mind, Varda embarked on several scouting trips to the south of France in fall 1984, usually alone.

The first concrete step Varda took in the making of *Vagabond* was to choose the setting: "[I] first chose the décor and the places, the land-scapes, the general impression. And next, the actors" ("Varda à Saisir."). Indeed, Varda spent far more time choosing locations for the film than writing a screenplay. Just as with *La Pointe Courte* and *Du côté de la côte*, Varda sought offbeat locations in the south of France. Several trips to the city of Nîmes and its environs solidified her desire to shoot in the Gard and Bouches du Rhône departments, regions that lack the easy charm of Provence or the Côte d'Azur but whose harsh winter landscapes, isolated villages, insular farms, and abandoned homes in-trigued her. While talking with farmers, shopkeepers, homeless people, runaways, hitchhikers, and other vagabonds, Varda slowly developed insight into the kinds of characters that would populate her film. There were ethical reasons, as well as practical ones, for Varda to engage in so much preparation. "It is not so much the film I'm preparing as myself. It is necessary to be close to this world of marginal people, at least for a while, to dare to speak of them as if one understands them" (Varda, *Varda par Agnès*, 168). Varda did not, then, assume that she necessarily understood the motivations or the daily conditions of drifters. She set about the preparation of the film as if she were an investigative reporter, interviewing farmers, villagers, and drifters.

As we have seen with her preparation of *La Pointe Courte*, the three documentary shorts she made in the late 1950s, and *Cléo from 5 to 7*, Varda was accustomed to finding inspiration for a film from a particular place, and she was also accustomed to conducting extensive research and location scouting in order to flesh out characters and action. With *Vagabond*, however, Varda intensified her preproduction research. She spent many months traveling through the south of France in the fall of 1984, sometimes with friends or assistants and sometimes alone, researching locations, people, and customs. This lengthy planning process resulted in changes in the film's focus. Initially, Varda had envisioned a plot with a male protagonist that would explore the interactions of eight people, some of whom were drifters (Alion 4). A chance encounter with a young woman on the road convinced her to structure the film around a female drifter (Varda, *Varda par Agnès*, 168). In the manner of the professor in the film, Varda happened to pick up a young hitchhiker and spent time with her, an experience that helped Varda understand the specific hardships for women of life on the streets. The drifter, Setina Arhab, stayed in Varda's home in Paris for a time and eventually had a cameo role in the film. This research process resembled nothing so much as a series of improvisations, conducted in the field, at the various sites where Varda envisioned filming.

The importance of place in Varda's working process and in her finished films cannot be overemphasized, as many have noted. Part of Varda's journey is regularly exploring a chosen region at length, waiting for ideas, emotions, and images to emerge. If her efforts first resemble a form of tourism (albeit one that is neither self-conscious nor superficial), it is difficult to imagine Varda not working to attain some level of indigenous knowledge or access, as she had during her extended travels in California. In a 1986 radio interview Varda spoke eloquently about this element of her creative process:

My working method is often as follows: alone, I look for or find places where scenes will be shot about which I know nothing, and people who will be secondary characters of a story I can scarcely imagine. The reality with which I inform myself liberates my imagination. Groups of shots are put into place, or an emotion invades me and dominates the scene yet to be invented: pride at having a lively and autonomous existence; uncontrollable sadness when night falls; a desire to speak to those who live in the area and to pierce the magical secrets of each wall, each door, each courtyard, each tree; the sudden fear of the violence of others; nostalgia for the lives of others as they're telling their stories; solitude among ruins; the desire to cry (Veinstein).

The importance of emotion and imagination in Varda's working process, rarely expressed with such detail, is only one element of her preproduction work. As a result of taking the time to wander the region and speak with its inhabitants, specific characters and themes emerged. At a blood donation truck, she met a garrulous ex-drifter who gave her the idea of shooting a scene in which Mona donates blood for food. She met several shepherds who had rejected a traditional existence in the wake of the political upheaval of May 1968 and were living in seclusion on a remote farm. One such shepherd ended up playing the philosophical goatherder who offers Mona some land to farm and a caravan to live in, but then, exasperated with her laziness, eventually turns her out. She met a garage mechanic who said he did not like female hitchhikers and created the role for him as the garage mechanic who hires Mona to work at his garage and later emerges from her tent, zipping up his pants. Varda came upon a newspaper article about contaminated plane trees that inspired her to develop the character of a university professor who would travel the region by car and pick up Mona. After speaking with hundreds of people she met on the road, in shelters, and in train stations, Varda began to envision concrete characters one might encounter on the road (Veinstein). More and more, her improvised encounters served also as auditions for the film taking shape.

The development of Mona progressed in several phases. At one point, Varda envisioned a film about two young men on the road who meet a young, rebellious woman (a socially engaged recasting of *Jules et Jim* or Bertrand Blier's *Les Valseuses / Going Places*, 1974). This version of the film would have initially followed the experiences of the three characters before shifting focus to the woman alone. But after her encounter with a female hitchhiker (Setina), Varda found herself intrigued by this rebellious and enigmatic young woman and decided to structure the narrative entirely around a solitary, wandering woman. Less interested in character psychology than in the protagonist's movements, sounds, and conversations, Varda wanted viewers to feel how a woman on the road survives day to day: "Where does one sleep? What noise do boots make on pavement, in a field, on gravel? What does one say to those one encounters outdoors: farmers at work, masons, mechanics or other vagabonds?" (Alion). Varda's desire to minimize traditional narrative procedures and instead maximize the visual qualities of the film is articulated in a note written to herself on January 23, 1985, shortly before the shoot began: "What is needed is *more* spectacle or image or the unexpected and *less* story, psychology" (Ciné-Tamaris, *Sans toit ni loi*). Varda underscored her resistance to character psychology as a causal element in *Vagabond's* narrative in a radio interview in 1986. When asked whether Mona "refuses" to take into account the cold that ultimately kills her, Varda retorts, "She does not refuse, she is there, it's cold, she dies because she no longer has a sleeping bag. For me, it's not philosophical, it's simple" (Veinstein). In other words, it is not Mona's motivations or actions or state of mind, Varda implies, that cause her death; rather, it is the material problem of (and the circumstances that led to) her lack of a sleeping bag that causes her death (Servat). Varda continues, "This is someone who does not want to talk, who does not want to communicate. Her way to refuse the world, more than to challenge or contest it, is to live dirty. . . . There is not a clumsy message there but rather a series of circumstances that befall a rather tough girl. Once she has lost her sleeping bag, which was her shell, and undergoes the final soiling, she can only fall and not get up" (Servat). It is a streamlining of narrative that hails back to her early Left Bank preoccupations with the *nouveau roman* and the circle of Duras and Robbe-Grillet, and it is no accident that the film is dedicated to Agnès' old friend Nathalie Sarraute, a key novelist in that movement.

By January 1985, with the screenplay still unwritten, Varda proceeded to cast the film and to secure funding. Repeating her strategy from her first fiction feature, *La Pointe Courte*, Varda employed both professional actors, including Sandrine Bonnaire, Macha Méril, and

Stéphane Freiss, and nonprofessional actors, such as Yahiaoui Assouna—who plays the vineyard worker—along with goatherders and the garage mechanic who plays a more unsympathetic version of himself (Alion 6). Varda envisioned seventeen-year-old Sandrine Bonnaire, celebrated for her performance of the rebellious teenage girl in Maurice Pialat's *A nos amours* (1982), in the role of Mona. Bonnaire accepted the part right away, but raising funds was more difficult.

According to notes in the production files for *Vagabond* at Ciné-Tamaris, Varda pitched the film to the typical funding sources, including film production and distribution companies (MK2, Gaumont) and cable and television companies (France's Canal+, Britain's Channel 4, and Germany's ZDF). But she was ultimately only able to convince the French television station Antenne 2 to contribute 10 percent of the budget in exchange for the right to broadcast the film on television. Eventually, MK2 came on board as the film's distributor, but only after *Vagabond* was accepted by the Venice Film Festival. Varda admitted later, "It must be said that when you talk about a dirty and rebellious girl who says nothing, or rather 'shit,' and ends up freezing to death in a ditch, you don't awaken the desires of the deciders" (Alion). After initial attempts to secure a producer and a distributer failed, Varda launched the shoot with funding from her own production company. Given the film's budget (around 6.5 million francs), the conditions of production were by necessity modest. The cast and crew lived together in a dormitory supplied by the city of Nîmes and normally used by visiting athletes (Alion 6).

The film was shot from February 25 to May 6, 1985. At the beginning of the shoot, in late February 1985, Varda had only a twenty-five-page script and fragments of dialogue. Her daily working method was as follows: early in the morning before each day's work, she wrote the precise dialogue for the day, read it aloud to an assistant, made necessary changes, and photocopied it before driving to the first location of the day. Echoing her initial emphasis on location shooting over the writing of a traditional screenplay, Varda's shooting method likewise foregrounded place over dialogue. The sheer number of locations used in *Vagabond* (thirty-seven) is also indicative of Varda's emphasis on place (Ciné-Tamaris, *Sans toit ni loi*).

Once the film was made, Varda's difficulties were not over. First, Unifrance, the government-sponsored organization charged with pro-

Cast and crew, *Vagabond* (1985).
© Ciné-Tamaris

moting French film abroad, declined to show *Vagabond* to the selection committee of the Venice Film Festival (Denoyan). Varda had to call the festival herself and ask the committee to view her film, which resulted in the acceptance of the film for the official competition. Still more persuasion was required to secure the film's distribution. On the eve of the Venice Film Festival, Varda still did not have a distributor for the film. She apparently called MK2 (the French distributor run by Marin Karmitz, who'd incidentally started as an assistant on *Cleo*) (Bouffard) and said, "You should probably take [my film] before I give a press conference and say that no one in France wanted it" (Denoyan). MK2 agreed to distribute the film just before Varda left for Venice.

Vagabond won the prestigious Golden Lion award at the Venice Film Festival, in spite of Unifrance's initial reluctance to submit the film. The French Syndicate of Cinema Critics also awarded *Vagabond* "Best Film" and Sandrine Bonnaire won a César for "Best Actress." The film attracted more than a million viewers in France alone and was a commercial success well beyond Varda's expectations. *Vagabond* has been shown in count-less retrospectives over the years and in 2004 was canonized, in a way, by official French culture. It was added to the list of required texts for the "Agrégation Interne de Lettres Modernes et Classiques," the competitive national examination taken by those who wish to attain the highest level of university professor or secondary school teacher.[11]

By the mid-1980s, Varda had retained certain strategies in her film-making practice but had added new ones as well. As we have seen, ex-tensive, almost improvisational location scouting and research, present in her working method since *La Pointe Courte*, were more important than ever to Varda at this stage of her career. *Vagabond*, although a film about a rootless character, is firmly rooted in the vineyards, farms, villages, and culture of the Languedoc region. Place—whether Sète (*La Pointe Courte*), the rue Mouffetard (*L'Opéra-Mouffe*), the 14th arrondissement (*Cleo*), Los Angeles (*Lions Love* and *Documenteur*), or her own rue Daguerre (*Daguerréotypes*)—is always foregrounded in Varda's work. The film also conforms to Varda's persistent interest in mixing the codes of fiction and documentary. *Vagabond*'s most obvious connection to real events and people was established by Varda's choice to use her recent awareness of people dying of exposure as the film's inspiration. The character of Mona is wholly fictional, but her opacity and physicality were nourished by Varda's encounters with the many marginal figures to whom she is persistently drawn. Varda's employ-ment of both professional and nonprofessional actors enhanced the film's connection to documentary, as did the numerous scenes using direct address or interview format, a style with close ties to both television reportage and documentary. The twelve tracking shots featuring Mona walking sometimes resemble the "dead time" one sees in observational documentaries by directors such as Frederick Wiseman, although the scenes' patterned quality, pictorial beauty, and music move them closer to the codes of European art cinema. The addition of the tracking shots late in the shoot underscores Varda's increasing willingness to improvise and remain flexible. Finally, the relentless effort required by an inde-pendent filmmaker to fund and distribute a relatively low-budget film had not changed from the mid-1950s to the mid-1980s, despite Varda's undeniable stature and global visibility as a filmmaker. In the years to come, Varda would continue to combine the codes of documentary and fiction film in yet new ways with *Jane B. par Agnès V* (1987), a playful and prismatic portrait of the actress and singer Jane Birkin, and *Jacquot de Nantes* (1990), a biographical film that mixes contemporary footage of a frail Jacques Demy near the end his life with staged footage representing his youth and clips from his films. It was not until 2000, however, that Varda would experience once again the commercial and critical success she had achieved with *Vagabond*.

Social Criticism and the Self-Portrait: *The Gleaners and I*

After *Vagabond* there followed several more short films and the feature-length portrait of Jane Birkin in midlife crisis, *Jane B. par Agnès V* (1986–87). There was also the fiction feature *Kung-Fu Master!* (1987), which starred Birkin as a forty-year-old woman who falls in love with a teenage boy (Mathieu Demy), a film that echoes Varda's earlier self-portraiture in *Documenteur* (which also featured a young Demy). It is also a story of a single mother, albeit much more provocative, taking as its subject intergenerational love and the incestual connections of mother-daughter rivalry. This was reinforced through the casting of Varda's son and Birkin's daughters Charlotte Gainsbourg and Lou Doillon (a provocation Birkin's former partner, Serge Gainsbourg, explored at roughly the same time in his duet "Lemon Incest" with daughter Charlotte).

Varda and Mathieu's father, Jacques Demy, reunited in 1988 but would have only two more years together. The 1980s had been a difficult decade for them as a couple, and much of Varda's film output, even harking back to her California sojourn in the late 1970s, seems to suggest a strong creative drive fueled by a productive melancholy, inspiration through isolation. There is a recurring affect in Varda's films and more specifically in her identification with her marginal protagonists and background figures, as if it were an image of herself that both captivates her imagination and directs her inquisitive, empathetic eye toward other places and people: the stories of forgotten landscapes and ways of life in *La Pointe Courte*, a pregnant woman overwhelmed and alone in the throng of *L'Opéra-Mouffe*, and Mona, the emblem of the ultimate abandonment of self-abnegation and failure of the social contract.

While not especially private about her own life nor prudish about sexuality, Varda has never spoken in detail of what led to her separation from

Demy. She has expressed envy and admiration (in *Beaches*) for friends who managed to stay together over many years. In any case, facing a lengthy illness that Varda only years later acknowledged was AIDS, Demy spent the last years of his life traveling a bit with Varda, looking at art and revisiting the world of his childhood on the Atlantic coast as preparation for his memoirs. In 1990, Varda embarked on *Jacquot de Nantes*, a biographical feature detailing Demy's childhood in Nantes. Although very ill by this time, Demy attended much of the shoot, supplying anecdotes and confirming the authenticity of Varda's re-creation of his childhood. The making of the film became their last shared act, in fact one of their only artistic collaborations, as if Demy and Varda had instinctively understood the incompatibility of their cinematic styles and missions for all those years, while retaining the greatest esteem for what the other achieved. Demy passed away in the fall of 1990, two weeks after the shooting was completed. In a sense, Varda never ceased mourning Demy, and for the next ten years she would process this grief through film projects that touched upon their shared passions, a sort of posthumous collaboration they had denied during his lifetime. She made two further documentaries in the early 1990s devoted specifically to his memory: *Les Demoiselles ont eu 25 ans* (*The Young Girls Turn 25*, 1992) and *L'Univers de Jacques Demy* (*The World of Jacques Demy*, 1993). In the mid-1990s, Varda made *Cent et une nuits* (*One Hundred and One Nights*, 1995), a star-studded comic homage to the cinephilia she shared with her filmmaker husband and one of her few critical and commercial missteps. Even her later installation work, such as *Les veuves de Noirmoutier* (*The Widows of Noirmoutier*, 2005) and her autobiographical documentary *The Beaches of Agnès*, resonate with identification in shared loss and isolation. Demy's death, and the renewed intimacy the couple achieved revisiting the Nantes of his youth, marked a new stage in Varda's journey, one that took her to the coastal Pays-de-la-Loire region, scavenging for new landscapes and people with stories to pique her interest, while continuing to seek out the ever-fading traces of Demy's work and life there.

Ten years after Demy's death, Varda rebooted herself as a committed documentarist, experimenting with new forms and modes of narration while asserting her place as a viable, even beloved, figure in international art cinema with *Les Glaneurs et la glaneuse* (*The Gleaners and I*, 2000) and its hour-long sequel, *Les Glaneurs et la glaneuses:*

deux ans après (*The Gleaners and I: Two Years Later*, 2002). *The Gleaners* would be Varda's first digital film, a feature-length documentary about the long-standing practice of "gleaning" in France, originally a desperate scavenging for remnants of crops after the main harvest had taken place, and more figuratively a form of grazing for table scraps and leftovers in a variety of contexts, both social and cultural. The film is a fast-moving, heterogeneous work, more road movie than agitprop. Varda manages to criticize industrial farming's wasteful production practices while maintaining a witty and improvisational tone. The backbone of the film consists of interviews of gleaners—from Paris to southern France to the island of Noirmoutier—who glean out of need or desire. We meet poor people who must supplement their diets with leftover produce from urban markets and rural fields, an environmentalist from Aix-en-Provence who forages in dumpsters in protest against waste, and artists who seek discarded objects for their work. Varda stumbles upon famed psychoanalytic theorist and winemaker Jean Laplanche, who is happy to tell Varda why gleaning has been outlawed in Burgundy, and another winemaker who is a descendant of cinema pioneer Etienne-Jules Marey. The film also contains brief segments touching on a wide range of subjects that have little do with gleaning but that, taken together, provide a portrait of the filmmaker: Varda's love of painting, observations about her aging body, and her fascination with her digital video camera.

Although one of the primary themes of *The Gleaners and I* is the scandal of waste and hunger in an era of industrial farming, the film does not seek primarily to invite the viewer's pity or outrage or to criticize directly those who perpetrate the waste. Varda's rhetorical project is not to lecture the viewer about the problems of waste or hunger, but instead to demonstrate through her filmmaking technique and her own on-camera persona the beauty and humanity in things, practices, and people that have been rejected or marginalized. Neither lecturing nor employing the observational strategies of a Frederick Wiseman or a Nicholas Philibert, Varda instead foregrounds authorial intervention and the strategy of digression. The film's constant, playful shift in attention from paintings of gleaners to practices of gleaning and to Varda's self-portraiture work simultaneously to encourage a way of looking at the world that rewards openness to unexpected encounters and a respectful curiosity about others. This of course is her way of looking at the world.

To understand how Varda accomplishes this, a closer look at the structure and the style of her film is crucial.

The film begins not with an exposition on the problem of hunger in contemporary France or with an analysis of the impact of industrial farming, but with a more personal image. Varda's cat, Zgougou, gazes off screen and then looks directly into the camera. Longtime fans of Varda's work are unlikely to be surprised by this choice of an opening image, for cats have long populated Varda's life and films. Indeed, the logo of Varda's production company Ciné-Tamaris is a cat's face. Zgougou seems to have been especially beloved, because she played a sizable role in Varda's short film *Le lion volatil* (2003) and would become the subject of "Zgougou's Tomb," one of Varda's installations in *L'île et elle* (2006). But for now, the cat's image is a whimsical introduction to a film that nevertheless purports to treat serious subjects such as poverty, and also serves to remind us of the extent to which the director's domestic environment is closely interwoven with her professional pursuits. This is a well-known facet of Varda's public persona dating back at least to *Daguerréotypes* (1976), a documentary whose subject was her neighbors, chosen in part because she needed to stay close to home with her son Mathieu, then a toddler.

The film's first two minutes demonstrate the heterogeneity of the film's themes and locations. Varda's cat is first perched imperiously on top of a computer whose screen reads "CINE TAMARIS presents" and is then revealed next to a large Larousse Illustrated Dictionary while we hear Varda's voice reading the definition of "gleaning." As the cat nuzzles the book, Varda mentions that dictionaries typically illustrate the definition of gleaning with a reproduction of Jean-François Millet's celebrated painting *The Gleaners*. We are shown the reproduction of the painting in her dictionary and then whisked to the Musée d'Orsay to see time-lapse footage of the original painting as well as the tourists who photograph it. Millet's painting was called *Des Glaneuses* in French, with the indefinite article, *Some Gleaners* (although often referred to with the definite article, "*Les*"), with the plural noun gleaners gendered as feminine. Varda's film title provides the neutral or masculine "*glaneurs*" and a single "*la glaneuse*," definite article, the gleaning woman, revealingly rendered in English as "and I." Millet offers a marginal vision of France's most *démunies*, or vulnerable, figures—impoverished laborers foraging for loose grains, with indications of menacing landowners or farmworkers guarding the completed harvest in the distant backround. The painting seemed to celebrate the lowest ranks of rural society (of which he himself was the issue) at a time when middle-class farmers were bent on denying them gleaning rights. For the largely upper- and middle-class patrons of art, the painting was an unwelcome commentary on France's social conditions in the restive years following the 1848 revolution (Kleiner 355). In Varda's next scene, an elderly woman standing at the edge of a plowed field speaks with nostalgia about her gleaning days and demonstrates the gesture of bending down, picking up wheat, and putting the wheat in her apron. Graphic matches are created between her gesture and the gestures of women gleaning in clips of silent film footage. Varda creates additional graphic matches between the archival footage and shots of two other paintings that feature female gleaners bending down to pick up wheat. Following the interview with the rural woman is an interview with a middle-aged, well-dressed woman who owns a café. She and her father gleaned during the war in order to eat, but they glean for fun now. The film's opening thus hints at the film's mixture of concerns: the personal (Varda's domestic environment), the aesthetic (the paintings, the old film clip, the relationships Varda creates between shots), and gleaning. Crucially, Varda waits to introduce the type of gleaning necessitated by poverty until she has established a playful, nostalgic tone.

To introduce the more somber topic of gleaning born of food scarcity, Varda uses a montage of brief shots of anonymous people, many of them elderly, picking up abandoned food scraps amid the trash after the close of an urban outdoor market. Graphic matches are used once again to link Varda's footage of rural gleaners with Millet's gleaners and finally with urban gleaners. Varda's voice-over works to further effect the smooth transition from a nostalgic to a more analytical view. Accompanied by the electronic violin instrumentation of a rap song that will soon fully emerge, she informs us that "Gleaning might be extinct but stooping has not vanished from our sated society. Urban and rural gleaners all stoop to pick up. There's no shame, just worries." Her voice-over then ceases and the rap song takes over the soundtrack. The music is highly percussive and aggressive, its lyrics written by Varda but performed by young, insistent voices conveying both empathy and anger about the plight of gleaners:

Yeah, yeah
it's bad, sad, man
to bend down is not to beg
But when I see them sway
My heart hurts
Eating that scrap-crap
They've got to live on shit-bits
They've got to frisk for tidbits
Left on the street, leftovers
Rough stuff with no owners
Picking up trash like the street sweeper
Zero for us, for them much better
They got to roam around to kill the hunger
It's always been the same pain
will always be the same game.

While Varda's voice-over conveys no anger or criticism, her use of music signals the social criticism and anger connoted by rap.[12] Not only does the type of gleaning portrayed here contrast with the more nostalgic gleaning represented earlier, but its style differs as well. The rapid editing pace of this montage counters the leisurely editing pace of the preceding and succeeding scenes.

The film's strategy of juxtaposing different types of gleaning is crucial to its avoidance of tired tropes from the tradition of politically critical documentaries. Mireille Rosello argues that *The Gleaners and I* is neither a "straightforward critique of wasting" nor a "triumphant hymn to quick fixes" nor, ultimately, even a nostalgic celebration of nineteenth-century gleaning (30). Instead, the film is nothing less than "a poetic and theoretical essay on how we define and represent refuse and waste" (Rosello 29). Claude Marcia likewise suggests that Varda manages to treat different kinds of gleaning without slipping into a conventional expression of glib compassion for those who must glean for food. The film, she argues, legitimizes and even ennobles marginalized populations due to its "mosaic" construction and the resulting absence of hierarchy (Marcia 43–48). Different types of gleaners are interspersed with one another throughout the film in no immediately discernible order. For example, the unemployed alcoholic finds himself, via editing, next to the famous chef who gleans herbs (44). Moreover, Marcia suggests, gleaners of all types are ennobled by being inserted into the film's tissue of visual references, mostly painterly or photographic. Figures that might be marginalized in another sort of documentary—the homeless, the alcoholic, the poor—are elevated by the film's insertion of them into a distinguished pictorial universe that includes the paintings of Millet, Jules Breton, Rembrandt van Rijn, and Rogier van der Weyden as well as the photographs of Etienne-Jules Marey (Marcia 44).

The film's autobiographical element likewise moves *The Gleaners and I* away from the realm of agitprop and toward the essay film, with its poetic and personal qualities. Varda makes her first appearance in the scene following the montage of the urban market gleaners. Initially, we return to aesthetic contemplation at a museum in the town of Arras in northern France, where we see the magisterial painting by Jules Breton, *La Glaneuse* (1877). The painting is unusual, we learn, because it features a solitary female gleaner as opposed to a group. A close-up of the painting's subject, a strong, proud woman carrying a huge bundle of wheat over her shoulder, is followed by a wide shot of Varda standing next to the painting. Varda, like the woman in the painting, is holding wheat. The shot emphasizes Varda's diminutive size by showing two tall men—museum guards, presumably—holding up a cloth behind her that provides an internal frame. Varda's voice-over announces the intended meaning of the shot: "There is another woman gleaning in this film, that's me." A medium shot then features Varda alone and no longer small; she fills the frame and looks directly into the camera. In an elegant movement, she drops the wheat held in her left hand and brings forth a previously hidden video camera in her right hand, which she points directly at the camera, filming the scene, eventually obscuring her own face entirely. More than a mere return to aesthetic contemplation, this scene asserts Varda's authorial status in a playful, yet emphatic fashion. Varda first establishes a visual connection between herself and the female gleaner by imitating the figure's pose. She then suggests her distance from the nineteenth-century peasant by isolating herself in the frame with the use of a medium shot and then, using a slow, dance-like gesture, substituting an ancient symbol of agriculture and nourishment for the latest in moving image technology: a small digital video camera. The scene suggests that like the woman in the painting,

Varda is a strong, solitary, working woman, but her work is the creation of moving images. In an era in which women are still underrepresented in the ranks of filmmakers, this is a powerful image indeed. Varda will take self-portraiture to a more intimate level in the subsequent scene, connecting it directly with digital video technology.

Leaving the museum, Varda enters a kind of abstract space in which she experiments with her camera's effects. Images of Varda's distorted, pixellated face are accompanied by her voice-over marveling at the capacities of the (then) new, small digital video cameras. Next, Varda combs her hair, exposing her gray roots, and she acknowledges that "my hair and my hands keep telling me that the end is near." Back in her car, traveling to another region of France, she shows her aging hands to the viewer once again, but then says, "Okay, for the moment we are driving toward Beauce, renowned for its wheat." The moment of reverie and contemplation is over; it's time to get back to work.

One function of the brief scenes featuring Varda's aging body is their implicit invitation to think broadly about what our culture accepts and rejects. Rosello's astute analysis of the film shows that the film's "parallel between filming and gleaning is increasingly exposed as asymmetrical," yet the film's connection between gleaning and old age makes increasing sense as the film progresses (35). Varda's close-ups of her own hand are a "fascinating mixture of self-centeredness and anti-narcissism"; the female body is "revealed but not unveiled," a representation of the female body that is quite at odds with those in conventional films (Rosello 35). By showing her gray roots and her imperfect skin, Varda "questions both the cultural definition of female beauty and the cultural imperative that makes beauty mandatory in our represented universe" (Rosello 35). In other words, while Varda could easily have represented herself in a more conventionally attractive fashion, she deliberately chooses to refrain from equating old age and beauty, making instead the more radical choice of searching for "new visual and narrative grammars of old age" (Rosello 35). The scene in the museum insists upon the fact of female authorship in cinema; this scene, even more radically, refuses the association of femininity with conventional beauty as well as the association of old age and infirmity. Varda shows us her aging body, but then moves on, demonstrating the pleasures of new technology and the value of turning one's gaze outward. The film suggests that our culture is too quick to reject slightly bruised apples, misshapen potatoes, and even women who don't conform to certain norms. By foregrounding the wrinkled and aging yet still curious and capable Varda, the film implicitly invites us to look again at what we tend to reject and reconsider its value. The film does not dwell in the realm of self-portraiture or the experience of aging for long. The following scene, perhaps the sole expository moment in the film, follows the trajectory of potatoes from harvest to abandonment. We learn from one farmer that he rejects twenty-five tons of potatoes from each harvest because they do not conform to the specific size mandated by grocery stores. The enormous waste is compounded when farmers fail to announce where and when they will dump their produce, causing the potatoes to quickly become green and inedible. Varda shows the absurdity of this practice and then demonstrates through her own actions how one might respond. In a heap of abandoned potatoes, she finds heart-shaped potatoes, which intrigue her. In a gesture of reflexivity, she has herself filmed while she films her own hand picking up heart-shaped potatoes. She then takes

Finding value in a rejected potato in
The Gleaners and I (2000). © Ciné-Tamaris

the heart-shaped potatoes home, displaying and cherishing them. The incident does not end, however, with aesthetic *détournement* (mis/appropriation); she gets the idea to tell a food charity organization called les Restos du coeur (Restaurants of the Heart) about the abandoned potatoes. She returns to the field with the organization's volunteers and documents their gleaning. In voice-over she says, "That day they collect almost 700 lbs. At least that's something." She may not be able to end waste or hunger, but she can at least help get the produce to those who need it.

Even this brief analysis of the film's structure reveals the diversity of gleaning practices Varda has chosen to document and the nonhierarchical way in which she treats them. More broadly, we can also see the diversity of documentary strategies employed. In some ways, her documentary is quite traditional. Like so many expository documentaries, she relies extensively upon interviews. We meet the gleaners themselves, the owners of the land where the gleaning takes place, and judges who explain the legal ramifications of gleaning. But Varda also uses strategies from poetic, reflexive, and interactive documentaries, including staging (such as when the singing children skip laterally in the foreground from right to left, ultimately framing their mother and sister in the center background), the repeated insertion of herself into the frame and onto the soundtrack, and her emphasis on the technology used to make the film, her lightweight digital video camera.

One consistent aspect of Varda's documentary practice is the use of a dominant organizational schema spiked with digressions. As we have seen, the chronological architectural history of *Ô Saisons, Ô chateaux* repeatedly gives way to mini-portraits of caretakers, gardeners, and fashion models; the exposition of the "exotic" tourist attractions of the Riviera in *Du côté de la côte* splinters into poetic reveries on sunbathing practices; *L'Opéra-Mouffe* weaves into its categories of people and things found on rue Mouffetard abstract portraits of vegetables and a poetic love story. Varda's longtime interest in combining structure and digression is intensified in *The Gleaners and I*, partly because of its "road film" structure. Instead of confining herself to one region or one street, Varda moves all over France, remaining open to encounters and events that might shift the focus of her film. The aleatory quality, visible in most of Varda's films, is enhanced here by Varda's choice to expand the film's setting to the entire country of France and to adopt a broad and nonhierachical definition of her subject, gleaning. This documentary, more than anything she had made thus far, foregrounds Varda's personal history, filmmaking methods, and ways of looking at the world.

Agnès Varda's working methods as a filmmaker, as we have seen, have shifted over time. At the beginning of her filmmaking career, she planned every shot and wrote every line of dialogue in advance. By the time she made *Vagabond*, she had shifted to a working method characterized by a mixture of careful planning and improvisation. Her working method for *The Gleaners and I* reveals an intensification of Varda's penchant for improvisation and also extends her career-long interest in interacting with her viewers. After she completed *Gleaners*, she began to prepare supplemental material about the film for its DVD release. One of the supplements, *Two Years Later*, became an hour-long documentary that was distributed on the *Gleaners* DVD and also released in cinemas and shown on television. Varda was inspired to create a longer work because viewers of *Gleaners* had written to her in unprecedented numbers, telling her of their own gleaning practices.[13] *The Gleaners and I: Two Years Later* revisits the people featured in *Gleaners* and provides updates on their lives, but it also showcases the films' viewers and their letters to her, thus extending Varda's traditional regard for her spectators' experience of her work to something resembling a conversation, or at least a satisfying exchange.[14] Analysis of the production, exhibition, and reception of *Gleaners* reveals the evolution of an unusual project, the changes that digital tools brought to Varda's work, and the intense response the film elicited from critics and ordinary viewers alike.

In fact, *The Gleaners and I* began as a very different project from the feature-length, theatrically exhibited documentary it became. A project description created by Varda in August 1999 proposes not a film, but a television series consisting of four segments lasting twenty-six minutes each (Ciné-Tamaris, Les Glaneurs et la glaneuse, "Projets Préléminaires"). The series, initially titled "The Gleaner's Basket or the 'Store-Magazine' of the Gleaner" ("La Sacoche de la glaneuse ou magasin-magazine de la glaneuse"), was initially proposed to Arte, the Franco-German television network. The initial proposal hints that the series would explore gleaning in a metaphorical fashion, showing the results of Varda's "wandering quest for images, sounds, meanings and surprises . . . grains of wheat . . . that one gathers for nourishment" (Ciné-Tamaris, Les Glaneurs et la glaneuse, "Projets Préléminaires" 1). Each of the four segments of the series would be shot at a different season of the year and would treat some themes "continuously" and others "discontinuously." Varda initially generated many categories of subjects to feature in the series, including mini-portraits of her friends and neighbors; cats, both real and those from her collection of ceramic, straw, wood, and porcelain cats; ordinary people who have famous names, such as a certain Jean Cocteau, who paints buildings for a living; shelves and cupboards in peoples' homes containing surrealist assemblages; and a baker who would make different kinds of bread in each segment. Other ideas proposed by Varda included continuing stories about the gradual development of an aspiring rock band and a mini-portrait of plants on a balcony that flower and then dry up over time. Yet another idea entailed the creation of portraits of mail carriers as well as people addicted to email, a theme that would underscore the satisfaction of transmitting words and establishing contact, regardless of the format. Another proposed section titled "Returning from Trips"—one of the few subjects retained in *Gleaners*—anticipated a voice-over exploring what remains after a trip and shows airline tickets, city maps, postcards, and gifts received. The overall goal, stated at the end of the proposal, was to "create and nourish curiosity for 'others'" (Ciné-Tamaris, Les Glaneurs et la glaneuse, "Projets Préléminaires" 9). I can think of few words that encapsulate better the overarching mission of Varda's entire career.

Even this preliminary proposal shows that Varda understood that the appeal of the work would not only be the people, places, and things she filmed, but the ways she wove the threads of her subject together: "The list is easy to draw up . . . but it's the assemblage, the proportion of the themes, their relationships to the thread and the fluidity of the montage that will eventually make the difference and the charm of this personal series" (9). Early on, it was clear that Varda's key goal would be to juxtapose in compelling ways a collection of disparate people, places, objects, and actions. At the end of the first proposal, she states, "To summarize my intentions, which I've delivered in part here, I would like, in a very personal way . . . to mix topic areas skillfully including daily life, the words of the French language, the love for an approach toward painting, anecdotes and some avatars of the everyday, faces, work, urban and rural landscapes" (8). The emphasis on urban and rural gleaners emerged only in later proposals, while a proposed section on painting, mentioned only briefly in the first proposal, was expanded over time and became a major theme of the finished film.

Varda's presence in *Gleaners* was anticipated from the beginning, but the nature of her self-presentation shifted as the project developed. One section of the proposal, humorously titled "And Me and Me and Me" (which cannot help but evoke singer/actor Jacques Dutronc's 1966 hit "Et moi, et moi, et moi," a verse of which intones "900 million dying of hunger, and me and me and me, with my vegetarianism, and all the whisky I can drink, I think of them and then I forget, *c'est la vie, c'est la vie*"), anticipates shots of a miniature video camera in Varda's hand followed by brief shots of Varda's other hand. Buttressing the idea of a subtle authorial presence is Varda's stated goal of creating a "subjective documentary" made by an *"auteur"* who would be "almost hidden but whose presence (through the look, by the questions, by the subjects) would provide the tone" (3). From the beginning, then, Varda knew that she would appear in *Gleaners* and that she would film herself with a small digital video camera. Initially, she envisioned her presence as discernible primarily through the stylistic choices she would make, but as time went on, she decided to make the aging of her body one of the film's subjects. In the second version of the proposal, under the category still titled "And Me and Me and Me," for example, one finds the following, prefaced with a question mark: "Perhaps the adventure of the metamorphosis of my hair . . . filmed from week to week . . . if not, what I can see of myself in filming myself while holding a new mini-digital video camera (where am I? and in what state am I wandering?)" (Ciné-Tamaris, Les Glaneurs et la glaneuse, "Projets Préliminaires" version 2, 5). Interestingly, the English title of the film cuts right through Varda's coy "glaneuse" and gets to the heart of the matter: "And I." Shots of Varda's graying hair and aging skin would ultimately be among the film's most compelling and remarked-upon images, as would the close-ups of her aging hands.

The various drafts of the proposal reveal other interesting changes in the developing project. *The Gleaners and I* began as a four-part series, then became a fifty-two-minute documentary and eventually a feature-length film that would be released theatrically and on television. The metaphorical use of the concept of gleaning became more and more specific, as Varda began to divide the work into different modes of gleaning (the retrieval of abandoned edibles in fields, surveying vineyards and bodies of water, recouping abandoned furniture in the streets, etc.) and to develop the theme of the rejected potato as an object of beauty.

Arte did not accept Varda's proposal for *Gleaners*; ultimately, Canal+ was the only company that bought the rights to the film before it was made (Varda, "La moissonneuse-battante"). Arte must have appreciated the cornucopia of ideas in the original proposal for *Gleaners*, however, because some of its elements would emerge in the documentary series it funded thirteen years later: *Agnès de ci de là Varda* (*Agnès Varda Here and There*, 2013). This five-part documentary series made for television chronicles Varda's travels around the world for her exhibitions and film retrospectives. Structured primarily around her encounters with art and other artists, the series provides a survey of contemporary art as well as a chronicle of Varda's conversations with famous and ordinary people alike. Varda frames each installment with a prologue made up of images of the pruning and rapid regeneration of a tree in her garden in Paris on the rue Daguerre, an idea reminiscent of the idea conceived for *Gleaners* in which Varda proposed the charting of the life cycle of plants on a balcony. An inveterate recycler, Varda never wastes ideas.

Varda began filming *Gleaners* in September 1999 and finished in April 2000. The shoot did not always go smoothly; Varda worked in fits and starts.

> At Christmas, I was a little discouraged. I talked about the film to those around me. Friends of friends always gave me leads I wouldn't have thought of. While waiting, I prowled a lot. I didn't know what I would find. . . . I set out, alone. I was in a state of receptivity. So I met people! After, I returned . . . with a camera. We were [a team of] two, three or four and we shot. Then I edited—that's where I imposed order—the commentary began to emerge and sometimes called for another shoot! My film got made . . . while being made. . . . I have a method of working that is extremely fluid. Because I have a head that thinks slowly. That dreams . . . I wanted to make an honest film. The people I filmed took a long time to approach. One cannot watch someone pick up fruit from the ground and eat it and go toward him to ask brutally, "Why are you doing that?" (Piazzo).

The protracted shooting period for *Gleaners*, then, was exacerbated by the length of time it took to find and gain the trust of her subjects, as well as her initial uncertainty about the film's overall shape.

During the eight-month shooting period, Varda and her assistants shot for a total of twenty-nine days in teams, working in blocks of four to seven days at a time (Varda, "Filming *The Gleaners*"). The use of a lightweight digital video camera provided Varda the chance to shoot intermittently but also autonomously. Although she employed cinematographer Stéphane Krausz to shoot the majority of the film, Varda often filmed for two to three hours at a time on her own, especially at the close of markets, between 2:00 and 4:00 PM. She estimates that she filmed twenty minutes of the eighty-two-minute film herself (Benoist).[15]

The ease of digital tools also allowed her to intersperse the various stages of filmmaking that are often kept separate in the making of films on celluloid, editing as she went along. She described her work rhythm in more detail: "I shoot for a week, I edit, I think, I start the commentary and I look for other gleaners, we shoot, we edit, I write, etc. Halfway through the editing, I asked [Joanna] Bruzdowicz to record her original music with

Varda and her lightweight digital video camera
during the making of *The Gleaners and I* (2000).
© Ciné-Tamaris

variations in style and length. During the editing is when it's necessary to work on the structure of the film and its rhythm and to analyze what is lacking and to highlight those who have been filmed" (Bouffard 22). Varda's method of interspersing the shooting and editing of the film also allowed her to clarify her goals through time, balancing the material about herself and others: "My intention became clearer to me throughout the shooting and editing stages. Little by little, I found the right balance between self-referential moments (the gleaner who films one of her hands with the other) and moments focused on those whose reality and behavior I found so striking. I managed to approach them, to bring them out of their anonymity. I discovered their generosity. There are many ways of being poor, having common sense, anger or humor" (Varda, "Director's Note"). Varda thought carefully about how to create a balance between her film's central subject, gleaners, and herself. Making a film about people who must scrounge for food required tact and time.

Like its production schedule, the funding and distribution of *Gleaners* is exemplary of small-budget filmmaking in the landscape of contemporary European cinema. As had been the case with *Vagabond*, the task of funding a film about marginalization and poverty was not easy. The film was presold to Canal+, the French pay-TV cable station established in the mid-1980s by then minister of culture Jack Lang. Canal+ has been crucial to the ongoing vitality of French art house cinema in the age of the blockbuster, because it is required to funnel a portion of its profits into French and European film production in exchange for a monopoly over the first round of film releases to television (Michael). *Gleaners* cost only 300,000 euros to make (just under $500,000) and was an unlikely success, attracting 120,000 viewers in France alone, winning prizes from critics and film festivals around the world, and eliciting an extraordinary outpouring of personal letters and gifts from the films' viewers to Varda.[16]

The history of the film's exhibition is also typical of Europe's art house sector's reliance on festival screenings and specialized cinemas. The first public screening of *Gleaners* took place in May 2000 in Cannes. Gilles Jacob, director of the Cannes Film Festival, saw thirty minutes of *Gleaners* while it was being edited, liked what he saw, and programmed it for the festival. The next step in the film's exhibition history was the broadcast of the film on Canal+ on July 6, 2000, the day before its theatrical release. The following day, *The Gleaners and I* was released theatrically in Paris in *art et essai* cinemas, including the Latin Quarter art house Saint André des Arts, which kept it for seventeen weeks. The film was also shown every day at noon at MK2 Beaubourg, one of the art houses owned by exhibitor Marin Karmitz, who had worked on *Cleo from 5 to 7* at the beginning of his career in film. The film also circulated in many small towns and villages throughout France, because the CNC paid for prints to be struck expressly for this purpose (Darke). Linking the circulation of *Gleaners* back to the postwar goal of making art accessible to all, Varda observed, "Rural audiences may number only between 40 and 80, but that was the idea. When I worked as a photographer with Jean Vilar at the Theatre National Populaire after the war the idea wasn't to reduce culture to the lowest common denominator but to bring people something that was intelligent, concerned, unusual and generous. That's what's happened with this film" (Darke).

Like many small-budget films, *Gleaners* benefited from exposure at film festivals around the world. It was requested by more than fifty film festivals and was screened, among many others, at festivals in Toronto (in September 2000), Chicago and New York (October 2000), Hong Kong (April 2001), and Poland (May 2001) (Bouffard 22). The film won approximately forty awards, including ones from the Montreal Festival of New Cinema, the Chicago International Film Festival, the Boston Society of Film Critics, the New York Film Critics Circle, and the Los Angeles Film Critics Association Awards. The French Syndicate of Film Critics awarded *Gleaners* "Best Film," an award usually given to a fiction film. The film was screened not only in traditional film festivals, but also in festivals devoted to human rights and ecology (Diatkine and Lefort). The film was distributed theatrically in several foreign countries as well, including the Netherlands, Japan, Australia, and the United States. The film was shown, either theatrically or in festivals, in nearly seventy countries and five hundred cities and towns (Diatkine and Lefort).

The critical reception of *Gleaners* was exceptionally positive. The American trade paper *Variety* reviewed the film at the Cannes Film Festival and, while acknowledging that the film is "not an obvious commercial proposition" and will therefore "find its most likely home in Eurotube slots," said that the film offers "a fascinating portrait" of "people who live on the fringes of society" (Kelly). Ernst Callenbach of

Film Quarterly reported, "This is a film of playful, magical delight and delicacy. Audiences applaud at the end; they're surprised and grateful to feel so good as they leave a theater" (46–49). Many reviewers listed the distinctive people Varda introduced in the film: "Eternally curious, fascinated by people she meets, the filmmaker flushes out unexpected people: an unemployed biologist who is a vegetarian and who eats fruits and vegetables leftover at the end of the market, a winemaker psychoanalyst" (Royer). Some reviewers mentioned the gleaners by name, often singling out Claude, the unemployed man living in a trailer, and François, the volunteer literacy tutor. Critics also typically established links between *Gleaners* and Varda's earlier work. In a particularly positive review, Serge Kaganski of the French cultural weekly *Les Inrockuptibles* drew connections between the film and Varda's earlier documentaries and fiction films: "*The Gleaners and I* is a new jewel in her rich and long filmography, a documentary as free and playful as *Mur murs*, an experience as open and aleatory as *Daguerréotypes*, a 'political' work as powerful as *Vagabond*" (28–32).

Varda's embrace of digital video specifically caught the attention of critics and film historians, causing some to see *The Gleaners and I* as the inauguration of a new chapter in her career, while others associated the film with Varda's existing tendencies. *Sight and Sound* saw a connection between Varda's use of digital video in the making of *Gleaners* and her use of a lightweight 16mm camera in the making of *L'Opéra-Mouffe* (Darke). *Les Inrockuptibles* similarly saw digital video as enhancing Varda's already existing tendencies: digital video is a technology that only reinforces Varda's propensity for "freedom" in her filmmaking practice and "proximity" to her subjects" (Kaganski 28). Echoing the idea of digital video facilitating the filmmaker's access to other people, a writer for the literary journal *Esprit* declared, "Varda uses digital as a privileged instrument for discovering the other. No more need for a big camera, two lights, a microphone and technicians. Put the camera on a table and the filmmaker remains in a tête à tête with the interlocutor" (Trémois). Others saw Varda's use of digital video as helpful in her "beautiful adaptation to the accidents in the field" (Benoliel 63), as well as a newfound capacity to film herself: "Varda discovers the wonderful advantages of a digital camera here, gives herself over to a few minutes of troubling introspection, understands that she can film her left hand with her right hand [and] reduce the distance between the two sides of the camera" (Kaganski 28). Art historian Homay King sees *Gleaners* as nothing less than an exemplar of a kind of digital cinema that is "materialist, feminist, phenomenological and political," a significant alternative to the dominant theoretical conception of digital arts as abstract or ephemeral (421).

Varda herself is careful to neither overstate nor ignore the importance of digital technology in her filmmaking practice: "What's missing in all this talk of digital technologies is the understanding that they're only tools to shoot and edit with, they're not ends in themselves. . . . For me, the DV camera and the Avid are tools I use to get closer to people more easily and to shoot on my own and to collapse the time lapse between wanting to film something and actually being able to do it" (Darke 30). At a roundtable discussion with several filmmakers on the impact of digital video, Varda further elaborated on her use of the technology, noting its links to reportage: "For example, I arrive just when something is happening: a guy is destroying televisions. There, it's the 'click-click' of the photographer's Leica. You have to be there at the right moment" (Frodon, "La caméra numérique"). And a digital video camera is useful as a kind of "notebook" for sketching out her ideas in solitude. She would never have asked a cinematographer to film her hands because "I wanted to look at them myself. There is a personal and immediate relationship [between the camera and my] impressions and thoughts" (Frodon, "La caméra numérique").

While digital video certainly allowed Varda to intensify her existing habit of establishing intimacy with her documentary subjects and engaging in personal, low-budget filmmaking, a more significant turning point in Varda's lengthy career was the creation of multimedia installations beginning in 2003. The humble potato, both a symbol of the excesses of industrial farming and a beloved found object in both of Varda's *Gleaners* films, would take center stage in her inaugural installation, *Patatutopia*.

From Cinema to the Gallery: *Patatutopia* and *L'île et elle*

December 2008: I am in Sète to see Varda's installations at CRAC (Centre Régional d'Art Contemporain) Languedoc-Roussillon. She has agreed to walk me through her latest exhibit, "La mer . . . etSETEra," and talk about each installation. We meet at the agreed hour, but she has a different idea: there's an exhibition nearby at the excellent Musée International des Arts Modestes that she insists I must not miss. Having looked forward for months to this privileged opportunity to hear Varda guide me through one of her installations while it is currently on display, I am nevertheless intrigued about this other exhibit, and accede to her obvious pride about this other "hometown" museum, which has begun to garner a decent international reputation. What is the exhibit? "Kitsch Catch," it turns out, which is devoted to . . . the culture of professional wrestling. Photographs, drawings, paintings, sculptures, collages . . . all devoted to muscular (or merely bloated) men in tights and hoods. I recall that Barthes wrote about "le Catch" in his *Mythologies*. There is nothing "beneath" Agnès Varda's voracious interest. I anticipate a forthcoming exhibit on the noble beauty of the body slam.

* * *

After nearly fifty years of work in photography, documentaries, and fiction films, in 2003 Agnès Varda inaugurated a new era in her career, that of the multimedia installation. Her first foray into installations was instigated by the prestigious Venice Biennale in 2003. Varda was invited to be part of *Utopia Station*, a large group exhibition curated by Swiss curator Hans-Ulrich Obrist, American art historian Molly Nesbit, and the artist Rirkrit Tiravanija. Varda contributed *Patatutopia*, a video installation exploring the forms of decaying potatoes. The experience offered Varda the opportunity to experiment with video and sculptural elements as well as to develop a new facet of her public persona: a visual artist-cum-*glaneuse* at home in museums, art fairs, and galleries.

One can easily understand Varda's attraction to the ethos of *Utopia Station*. The organizers aimed to create a neighborhood environment in which people could both engage with art and connect with one another. The press kit for the exhibition describes it as "a way station, a place to stop, to look, to talk and refresh the route." The curators of the exhibition conceived of utopia as taking multiple forms and carrying the possibility of positive action: "Utopia itself, an idea with a long history and many fixed ideologies, has loosened up to become a catalyst first, or the no-place it always was, a hope for the better future." *Utopia Station* sought to create a positive social environment in which one could experience art but could also get clean, nap, or listen to a live radio broadcast: "Utopia Station presents itself as a functional neighborhood open to social interaction, complete with a garden with funky communal showers designed by Tobias Rehberger, Padre de la Fontana (Father of the Fountain, 2003), ecological toilets designed by Atelier van Lieshout (Scatopia, 2002), its own web radio station (Zerynthia, in collaboration with Franz West), and a stilted hut where one might take a quick nap should it all become too exhausting (Billboardthailandhouse, 2000, by Alicia Framis)" (Jürgensen).

Varda's contribution to this large and multiform exhibition, *Patatutopia*, was made up of three videos, each lasting three minutes and thirteen seconds, projected simultaneously in a loop on large screens forming a triptych.[17] The videos featured images of potatoes with gnarled roots, rendered abstract and strangely beautiful in their process of decay. The soundtrack featured a variety of sounds, including ambient noise, music, and sounds of breathing. In addition to the videos, the installation contained sculptural and performance elements: Varda covered the floor of the exhibition space in Venice with 1,500 pounds of potatoes.

Varda's first installation: *Patatutopia* (2003).
© Ciné-Tamaris

A bench was available for viewers who wished to sit and contemplate the work. In addition to the moving images and the potatoes, there was a performative element to the installation. Standing at the entrance to her "potato shack" and dressed in a potato costume that emitted an audio recording of a recitation of different varieties of potatoes, Varda played the role of "Dame de Patate" (Lady Potato). Later, after the exhibition's opening, Varda placed a stand-in for herself, a mannequin dressed in the potato costume and displaying a photograph of Varda's face, a cat's face, or the mosaic self-portrait Varda created in 1953. This performative element of Varda's contribution to the show was not out of place: throughout the six-month life of the exhibition, many speakers, dancers, and musicians performed at Utopia Station. *Patatutopia* thus offered the visitor an unusual mixture of objects and experiences: austere images of sprouting, rotting potatoes, copious amounts of fragrant organic matter in the form of hundreds of potatoes, and the humorous, fairground-attraction-like presence of Varda herself.[18]

Varda's installations both echo her films' narrative and stylistic preoccupations and extend her work into new subjects, forms, and techniques. *Patatutopia* can easily be seen as an extension of Varda's films in several ways. She had already developed the potato motif extensively in her films *Gleaners* and *Gleaners: Two Years Later*, first exploring the waste involved in industrial farming through the rejection of nonstandard potatoes and then finding beauty in the misshapen and rejected potatoes. She had also, of course, made nonnarrative experimental short films, including *L'Opera-Mouffe* (1958), *Uncle Yanco*, and *7 P., Cuis., S. de b. . . . (à saisir)*. Moreover, Varda had long been in the habit of recycling characters, themes, and objects from one work to the next, with the subsequent work taking a completely different form, style, or mode of production. *Vagabond*, for example, featured some of the same actors and characters as *7 P., Cuis., S. de b. . . . (à saisir)*, while *Ulysse* (1982) explored the impact of a photograph Varda had taken many years earlier. Nor would this type of recycling end with *Patatutopia*. Varda would eventually transform the videotaped portraits of women in her installation *Les Veuves de Noirmoutier* (*The Widows of Noirmoutier*) into a documentary for the French cable channel Arte, before undertaking the most elaborate act of recycling of her career in *The Beaches of Agnès*, an autobiographical documentary feature that relies heavily upon clips of her previous work. On top of all that, potatoes, as one of the chief exports of the aforementioned Noirmoutier, fit perfectly with her post-Demy nostalgia/hagiography and her voluntary periods of exile to the Atlantic coast.

Despite the obvious links between *Patatutopia* and Varda's earlier contemplation of the potato in *Gleaners*, the making of her first installation nevertheless marks a radical new stage in her career, or at least a distinct awakening to dormant talents. First, *Patatutopia* was Varda's first move away from the standard exhibition practice of the projection of a feature-length film onto a single screen in a cinema. With the Venice Biennale commission, she relished above all the chance to configure and exhibit images and sounds differently, in a way that departed from cinema's single screen and theatrical viewing conditions.

> [The installation] allows one access to an apparatus where images and sounds are presented totally differently from those of a film. I had always worked . . . with flat images. Here, the fact of having three screens that surround is a bit disturbing for the viewer. We only have two eyes and this frustration of not being able to see everything produces a dynamic kind of looking. One goes from one side to the other, one is lost, but happy; that's what I wanted. (Régnier)

As we will see in the discussion of *L'île et elle* (2006), Varda's experimentation with multiple screens would carry over to projecting images across multiple screens, to placing screens in nonstandard places and configurations, and to choosing nonstandard material for the screen itself.

The making of *Patatutopia* also provided Varda the opportunity to think about change in organic material over a long time, a process which in turn allowed her to contemplate the passage of time and the creation of beauty from aging, abandoned objects. With her characteristic openness regarding her working methods, Varda describes the process of making *Patatutopia*:

> I gathered these potatoes from fields in September 2002. I also asked farmers to keep potatoes in the form of a heart for me. I put them all in boxes, in different containers, and I put them in my cellar. And, starting in March, I was able to see the result of nature and germination. I started to film certain potatoes, while working with the time of this germination. I filmed for a month and a half according to what came out of the potatoes. It's an organic,

not intellectual, work. It was working with the time of the cellar, the time of the darkness, the time of the potato. In the light, certain sprouts were translucent, very beautiful. It was very pleasurable to pursue this process of time, of aging. Germination reconnects us to old, rotten, useless, inedible things. Here, there is no narration, only the pleasure of filming. (Régnier)

Varda's description of her creative process with *Patatutopia* underscores the pleasure she takes in the act of creation, but also the specific appeal and the relative ease of creating installations. In contrast to feature film production, which usually requires a script, cast and crew, and at least a minimal budget, Varda was able to work on *Patatutopia* at home, simply and modestly, over a long time, filming and editing her subject, creating the soundtrack, securing the potato costume, and overseeing the installation of the screens and the projectors in the exhibition space. The pace, budget, and conditions for creation of the installation were significantly less onerous than those required for making a feature film.[19]

Finally, the making of *Patatutopia* allowed Varda to expand her network of collaborators and fellow artists by entering a new milieu, that of the international art fair. *Utopia Station* contained more than sixty works by individual artists, groups, and architects and more than a hundred posters commissioned by artists from around the world, including works by prominent artists such as Annette Messager, the French installation artist; Steve McQueen, the British installation artist and filmmaker; Patti Smith, the American musician, artist, and writer; experimental filmmakers Jonas Mekas and Carolee Schneemann, and installation artist-celebrities Tino Sehgal, Yoko Ono, and Marina Abramovic. Long a student of art history and an observer of developments in contemporary art, Varda now joined the ranks of artists she admired, and who understandably admired her.

Varda is not the only francophone filmmaker to have exhibited in galleries, museums, and art fairs.[20] Chris Marker made several multimedia installations from 1990 to 2008, and Chantal Akerman has exhibited her installations in galleries and museums all over the world since 1995. In 2006, contemporaneous with Varda's *L'île et elle*, Godard exhibited his own suite of installations, *Travel(s) in Utopia, Jean-Luc Godard 1946–2006, In Search of a Lost Theorem* at the Centre Georges Pompidou.

In an era in which it has been difficult for independent filmmakers to get financing and distribution for feature-length fiction films, it is not surprising that film directors already inclined to experiment have begun making installations; not only are they cheaper than feature-length films, they also allow filmmakers to experiment with new tools and attract new audiences.

Patatutopia was only the beginning of Varda's career as an installation artist. In 2005, she had her first solo show at the Galerie Martine Aboucaya in Paris. *3+3+15 = 3 Installations* featured a new version of *Patatutopia* as well as two new works, *The Widows of Noirmoutier* and *Triptyque de Noirmoutier* (*The Triptych of Noirmoutier*). Emphasizing Varda's interest in the possible configurations of the screen, the title of the latter piece refers to the number of screens used in the individual works. *Patatutopia* and *The Triptych of Noirmoutier* both used three connected screens that formed a triptych, while *The Widows of Noirmoutier* contained fifteen screens, one large screen surrounded by fourteen small screens. Both works would appear in her most ambitious show to date, *L'île et elle*, commissioned by the Cartier Foundation and exhibited in Paris in the summer of 2006.

Varda's participation in the Venice Biennale, while considered a successful debut, was an altogether modest intervention compared to the monumental *L'île et elle*. The Cartier Foundation, which commissioned the exhibition, is one of the most prestigious venues for the exhibition of international contemporary art. After opening in a space near Versailles in 1984, the Cartier Foundation moved to Paris's 14th arrondissement (fortuitously just a stone's throw from Varda's beloved rue Daguerre) in 1994 upon the completion of its twelve-thousand-square-foot, light-filled glass and steel structure designed by Jean Nouvel. The foundation mounts theme-based group shows but is especially known for its commissioning of solo shows from individual artists. In 1999, for example, the foundation turned over its ground floor to American installation artist Sarah Sze for the construction of a massive site-specific work, *Everything That Rises Must Converge*. In 2004, the foundation commissioned Raymond Depardon, a photographer and documentary filmmaker, to make a series of films, each devoted to one city. David Lynch's 2007 *The Air Is on Fire*, showcased Lynch's drawings, paintings, and photographs.

Each of the eight installations in *L'île et elle* refers to some aspect of Noirmoutier, an island off the Atlantic coast of France in the Vendée Department of the Pays-de-la-Loire region. The title deploys the kind of wordplay Varda revels in, literally "the island and she" (or her), but simultaneously evoking in French "il et elle" (he and she). The island, known for its scenic views, its sea salt, and its hand-harvested *bonnotte* potatoes, is where Jacques Demy went camping as a child. In the early 1960s, Varda and Demy bought and restored an abandoned windmill on the island. Noirmoutier became a sanctuary for Varda, Demy, and their children, a place to which they often retreated for periods of both rest and intense creative activity, such as when Varda filmed *Les Créatures* (1966) on the island. *L'île et elle* represents the island with whimsical, personal, and often melancholic images: there are playful video images of children playing on the beach (in *Ping Pong*); a giant, humorous re-creation of a 1950s-era postcard (*Grande Carte postale*), and an installation (*Tombeau de Zgougou*) representing the grave of Varda's beloved cat, Zgougou, who is buried in the back yard of Varda's home on the island. The installations exhibit Varda's long-standing preoccupations with the specificity of place, the experience of both human solitude and community, and experimentation with cinematic time, space, and composition.

That the exhibition's organizing element is a particular place should not surprise us. Since the very beginning of her work as an artist, Varda had been profoundly preoccupied with the specificity and importance of place. We've seen this extensively with *La Pointe Courte* and with the short documentaries Varda made in the late 1950s in the Loire Valley and the French Riviera, not to mention her Parisian ambles in *L'Opéra-Mouffe*, *Cleo*, and *Daguerréotypes*. In *Vagabond* (1985) Mona is defined precisely by her displacement, her lack of enduring connection to places or people, as she wanders through the south of France during one cold winter. *L'île et elle* then offers an exploration of Noirmoutier's landscape and a series of portraits of its residents. In the project proposal Varda created while planning *L'île et elle*, the first paragraph states her motivation clearly: "I would like to work on site in Noirmoutier, like painters who work on the ground. This island, which I know very well and have known for a long time, offers me landscapes, scenery and skies that inspire me as much as the local situations and people who live there."

Woven through the exhibition's main subject of Noirmoutier's land-scape and people are multiple aesthetic projects, including the exploration of ways of configuring time and space using moving images with sculptural elements; the various combinations of architecture and photography; and the screen in its myriad sizes, forms, and configurations.[21] Time and space come to the fore most notably in the installation *Le Passage du Gois* (*The Gois Passage*). Until 1971, when a bridge was built connecting the mainland to the island of Noirmoutier, one could only reach the island by boat or by a submersible paved road called the Passage du Gois. Twice a day, the two-mile long causeway emerges during low tide, allowing drivers, bicyclists, or pedestrians to cross over. The tide comes back in quickly; dawdlers occasionally have to seek refuge on the wooden platforms placed along the road and wait until the next low tide. Varda's *Le Passage du Gois* recreated this spatio-temporal constraint. The work, made up primarily of a time-lapse video of the Passage du Gois projected onto a heavy plastic curtain, was situated on the ground floor of the Cartier Foundation at the base of a flight of stairs. Poised at the entrance to this piece was an official placard listing the times of high and low tide. If one reached this installation at "high tide," the rest of the exhibition was temporarily inaccessible due to a mechanical bar that prohibited the viewer's further passage. Visitors were required to wait and watch a six-minute projected digital video of the ocean moving through its cycles at high speed. At "low tide," the barrier rose and the viewer walked through the "screen," a translucent curtain, into the next part of the exhibition. Visitors were thus at the mercy of the tides (or rather, Varda) in the sense that their trajectory through the show was determined by something other than their own desires and curiosity.

Another important motif of *L'île et elle* was the conjunction of architecture and photography. Inspired by corrugated steel structures used by fishermen on the island of Noirmoutier (as she had been in *La Pointe Courte*), Varda had several small cabins, or "shacks" as she refers to them, constructed for the exhibition. *La Cabane aux portraits* (*The Portrait Shack*), for example, was a large wooden cabin with a corrugated metal roof housing sixty photographic portraits of the island's residents. The men and women were segregated; there were thirty portraits of women on one side of the cabin and thirty portraits of men on the other. Each image, "portrait-collages," as Varda calls them, consisted of three distinct parts: a person looking directly into the camera, an internal frame placed behind each figure made up of either a photograph of the beach or of a boat, and finally the actual landscape in which the subject stood while being photographed. The landscapes were varied and included the beach, fields, the market, and a chateau; they did not necessarily offer clues to the subject's occupation or social context. Varda's varied approach to displaying her subjects here recalls the mix of "testimonial" styles in *Vagabond*, which shows just how early in her career she was thinking in nonlinear terms of multichannel narration. There is a sense in which even the parallel story lines of *La Pointe Courte* gave early evidence of Varda's aptitude for producing meaning on several planes, in several different places and moments, with varied duration. In the catalogue for the *L'île* exhibition, Varda emphasizes her method of working in the open air, of approaching people and asking them to pose for her, and of choosing to forgo the ease of Photoshop in her composition and construction of background imagery (Varda, *Agnès Varda: L'île et elle*, 43). As spectators, we are left with fleeting impressions of the people and settings of Noirmoutier, of Varda's respectful gaze toward the island's residents, and of the layered quality of the compositions.

An altogether different combination of architecture and photographic image occurs in *Ma Cabane de l'Echec* (*My Failure Shack*), a structure whose walls are made not of wood, but of strips of film. The strips of film were taken from a release print of *Les Créatures*, a fiction feature Varda shot on the island of Noirmoutier in the fall of 1965 in which Catherine Deneuve and Michel Piccoli play a couple living together on the island. The husband strolls around the island, seeking inspiration for the novel he is trying to write, while his pregnant wife, rendered mute after a car accident, prepares for the birth of their baby. Slowly the novelist's daily reality melds with the world of the novel he is creating. The film, an unusual mixture of art cinema and science fiction, did not fare well critically or commercially, but Varda recycled the "failed" film by creating an installation that viewers could experience in a number of ways.

As film theorists or historians, viewers could contemplate the materiality of the cinematic apparatus or Varda's reflexive gesture of displaying celluloid, the basic material of cinema, in a new way and in a new setting. As fans, they could scrutinize up close the thousands of frames containing the tiny faces of Deneuve and Piccoli, who in 1966 were icons of the French New Wave but by 2006 were synonymous with the variety and prestige of a much broader spectrum of French commercial and art cinema. Viewers who were not particularly conversant with the history of French cinema could explore the installation's plastic qualities by wandering in and around the cabin, sitting on a stack of metal film cans located inside the cabin, and observing the variable quality of the light filtering through the celluloid as a result of the Cartier Foundation's glass walls. Near the cabin Varda displayed an editing table, meant to evoke a dining table.

The other major preoccupation of *L'île et elle* was the moving image screen in its multiple guises. In *Le Tombeau de Zgougou*, an installation combining video and a large mound of sand, Varda eschewed both the traditional cinema screen and the TV "box" so common in video

Recycling a "failed" film: *My Failure Shack* (2006).
© Ciné-Tamaris

Catherine Deneuve and Michel Piccoli visible in
the strips of celluloid from *Les Créatures* (1966) in
My Failure Shack (2006). © Ciné-Tamaris

installations by creating a different sort of screen, one that appeared
to stretch along the floor and up a wall. In fact, two video projectors
mounted on the ceiling created this homage to Varda's cat, who died on
Noirmoutier in the summer of 2005: one projector sent moving images
to the floor, directly onto the mound of sand representing Zgougou's
tomb; another projector screened images onto the wall behind and
above the "tomb." The two images were seamlessly connected where
the wall met the floor. The video, which lasted three minutes and
forty seconds, consisted of footage of Zgougou, including a selection
of cameo roles across the Varda and Demy filmography. Next the
video related the decoration of the feline's grave. Pixellated images
of painted shells and brightly colored flowers accumulated, decorat-
ing the mound of sand. On the stone wall behind the grave was video
footage of climbing flowers. After the decoration of Zgougou's grave
was complete, Varda's camera soared high into the air. Moving far
above this minuscule grave, which was further embellished by a giant

paper flower placed in a nearby tree, the shot was initially taken with a crane, and eventually from a helicopter. Finally, a satellite image of the island took shape. The dramatic camera movement and the increasingly extreme shot scale emphasized the cat's relative insignificance in the larger universe, and yet the installation reinforced the importance of this tiny animal in the lives of so many. This cat, one intuits, was worth the expenditure and technical know-how on display. As in *La Cabane de l'Echec*, Varda transformed elements from her work in cinema into an installation that allowed her to explore new materials and new forms. Like *Passage du Gois*, when Varda projected time-lapse video images onto a transparent plastic curtain that viewers could later walk through, *Le Tombeau de Zgouzou* allowed Varda to experiment with the shape, size, and location of the screen. A screen need not be in the shape of a square or a rectangle and it need not be affixed to, or made up of, a wall. A screen could be a mound of sand on the floor.

Varda's use of multiple moving image screens in nonstandard sizes, forms, and configurations can be seen again in *La Grande Carte postale ou Souvenir de Noirmoutier* (*The Great Postcard or Souvenir of Noirmoutier*). Upon first glance, this installation appeared to be a gigantic, deceptively simple photographic image evoking a 1950s pinup postcard of a nude woman reclining on the beach. The work initially cited the tourist cliché of the holiday maker on Noirmoutier, but then offered something else. Intermittently, a black and white photographic image of another woman appeared, possibly depicting a corpse, superimposed over the pinup's body. In addition, there were small doors scattered over the surface of the large photographic image that concealed video images. Viewers could choose to open the doors, thus multiplying the viewing surfaces of the work. The video images hidden inside the doors revealed the drowned body of a fisherman floating in the water, a bird covered with oil, and a human hand whose fingers raked the sand. Yet another video featured scatological practical jokes performed by children. Once again, as in the larger image of the pinup, we have two registers here: somber reminders of loss along with signs of plentiful wit. An autobiographical element persists here yet again: the hand raking the sand is an excerpt from Varda's *Jacquot de Nantes* (1991) and is the hand of Varda's late husband, Jacques Demy, filmed near the end of his life on Noirmoutier. The blond pinup, whose face is that of Varda's daughter, Rosalie, and the anonymous drowned sailor coexist with the poignant footage of Demy near the end of his life. *The Great Postcard* offers both a celebration of summer at the beach, with its promise of beautiful bodies and children's play, and also the knowledge of death.

The multiple-screen *Triptyque de Noirmoutier (The Triptych of Noirmoutier)* referenced Varda's installation *Patatutopia* in its use of three connecting screens, but offered a more complicated conception of space and screen. *The Triptych of Noirmoutier* consisted of three screens, a large screen in the middle and two smaller screens on the sides. There were wooden shutters on the sides of the screens that allowed viewers to cover the smaller screens and view only the center screen. The center screen featured ten-minute loops of a man, his elderly mother, and his wife. The three people move quietly about the kitchen or sit at the table. The man sips beer, the elderly woman ties knots, and the middle-aged woman peels potatoes. Occasionally, the figures move "off-screen," that is, off the center screen and into the contiguous spaces of the side screens, which include a beach landscape on the left and a room containing a china cabinet on the right. Sometimes the characters move from these three spaces off-screen altogether. We have, then, an expansion of the cinematic idea of "off-screen space" into "multiple-screen" space. Moreover, this installation seemed to promise a narrative but then withhold it. The "characters," apparently a domestic unit, move about the rooms, silently and contemplatively. The installation presented the setting and characters of a family melodrama but occluded overt drama, emphasizing instead the economy of the actors' gestures and the passage of time. The installation suggested that the repetition of domestic tasks or the enclosure of the family home creates boredom and even melancholy, relieved only by an occasional visit to the beach. Here, as with *Passage du Gois*, *Le Tombeau de Zgougou*, and *La Grande Carte postale*, Varda invited subtle, sometimes conflicting, emotional responses while playing with multiple configurations of the screen, offering a shifting experience of duration and an expansion of traditional cinematic space.

Varda's experimentation with multiple screens is yoked to narrative and emotion even more clearly in the exhibition's final and most elaborate installation, *Les Veuves de Noirmoutier* (*The Widows of Noirmoutier*). A large screen in the center projects footage shot in 35mm of women, the eponymous widows, dressed in black. They walk, slowly and contemplatively, around and beyond a kitchen table placed on the beach. Surrounding the large, central screen are fourteen smaller screens containing digital video images. In the room are fourteen chairs and headphones that allow visitors to sit down and listen to each individual widow's story. Viewers choose a seat, put on the headphones, and listen to one widow at a time talk about what it was like to lose her husband and what her life is like now. The women seem unaccustomed to talking about grief, but Varda succeeds at drawing out telling anecdotes from each that communicate succinctly the experience of surviving one's husband and learning to live alone. Varda's identification is inescapable—she too is a widow of Noirmoutier.

We are accustomed to the respectful and empathetic regard for marginalized people in the films of Agnès Varda. *La Pointe Courte* offered a distanced look at both the inhabitants of the village of Sète and the troubled couple from Paris. *Daguerréotypes* provided limited but meaningful access to the lives of Varda's neighbors, the shopkeepers on the rue Daguerre with whom she herself identified. *Vagabond* was a veritable treatise on the politics and the complexity of looking at the "other," in this case a woman who travels from place to place, committing to no one, revealing

The Widows of Noirmoutier (2006).
© Ciné-Tamaris

little of herself. *The Gleaners and I* constructed respectful and sometimes witty portraits of people—artists, a chef, an alcoholic, a volunteer literacy teacher—who scavenge for a variety of reasons. Varda is gifted at creating complex characters that are both marginal and deserving of our sympathy, yet she keeps her distance and never lets us forget about the intricacies of watching and judging others. *Widows* extended this strand of her work by recounting the stories of rural widows, a population whose stories do not often get told, while at the same time foregrounding the importance of the apparatus used to convey these stories.

Here, more than in any of the other installations in *L'île et elle*, Varda relies upon narrative. It is as if one took the face-on portraits from the *The Portrait Shack*, placed them in domestic settings like those of *The Triptyque of Noirmoutier*, and gave them movement, voices, and stories. The widows, both young and old, recount their experiences of grief and solitude. But we also learn many details about how people on Noirmoutier live. The interviews often emphasize the centrality of fishing to the island's economy and culture—most of the lamented husbands were fishermen. One woman mentions that even before her husband died, she was used to solitude: "He was a sailor's sailor [*marin-marin*]! When my husband went out to sea, I was an auxiliary widow." Another widow speaks of the incessant work associated with fishing and the harvesting of sea salt. "We were outside day and night." Another portrait reveals with unexpected poignancy the material difficulties of a widow's life. One woman has recently been widowed for the second time. Her first husband died thirty years previously, at a time when she had three young children and was pregnant with a fourth. "We were living in poverty, we had nothing to eat, nothing at all." Intertwined with this unveiling of the material circumstances of the widows' lives are revelatory glimpses into the nature of grief.

Many of the widows have been alone for decades, while for some the grief is still fresh. One young woman recently buried her husband on the day of their first wedding anniversary. "[T]he house is still full of the presence of Thierry, of his smell. . . . Two days ago we ate green beans that he bought at the market. It's so recent. And you'd like to think that he's going to come back, that it was a joke." Some admit that their marriages were difficult: "I always knew that he loved me, but I often found that he loved me badly." One widow mentions the guilt she carries because her husband committed suicide. Another woman speaks of the difficulty of donating her husband's organs; she couldn't bring herself to give away his heart and she regrets it now. The interviews are brief, just three or four minutes long, but they manage to capture both the singularity and the similarities of the women's experience of widowhood. Varda recounts her own widowhood a bit differently. She eschews the interview format and begins with a carefully composed long shot of two chairs on the beach at low tide. She sits in one chair while the other remains empty, marking the absence of Jacques Demy, who died in 1990 at the age of fifty-nine. A medium close-up makes more apparent the sadness in Varda's expression. Next there are shots of seaweed on the beach and the sea itself. The camera then tracks right to the empty chair once again, and then to Varda, who is wearing different clothes than in the first shot. She is crying this time. There are more shots of seaweed on the sand, moving in the wind and then Varda's voice is heard, in voice-over, singing "Démons et merveilles" ("Demons and Wonders"), a poem written by Jacques Prévert and set to music by Maurice Thiriet for Marcel Carné's *Les Visiteurs du soir* (1942). While Varda sings, we see video footage of Demy taken near the end of his life on the beach in Noirmoutier, footage used also toward the end of *Jacquot de Nantes* (1991, the film she made just before her husband's death). What we hear connects loosely with what we see: the beach, the sea, the breeze, seaweed, and a close-up of Demy's face: "Demons and wonders / winds and tides / In the distance already the sea has withdrawn / And you like a piece of seaweed / Gently caressed by the wind / You stir dreaming." It is as if words cannot express Varda's grief; instead, the empty chair, her facial expression, and the singing of a song alongside the empty chair must suffice. This is the "he and she" of the exhibition's title, a community of shes signifying—through different stories, gestures, and ways of looking—their missing hes.

The experience of this installation is both public and private. Visitors to the gallery listen to each widow's story privately, while wearing headphones, but they sit in public, next to other viewers who listen to other stories. While viewers are absorbed in the semiprivate world of a particular widow's story, they can also watch the center image of widows moving around the empty dining table on the beach and also see (but not hear) the faces of the other widows on the small screens. While we watch the small screens and listen to the individual interviews, we never lose sight of the black-clad widows in the center, a mechanism that allows us to move back and forth from the particular to the general, from the modest to the grand, and from video to cinema. This configuration invites the viewer to contemplate the universality and also the particularity of grief, as well as the sensation of being part of a community, yet ultimately and paradoxically alone.

The Widows of Noirmouter retains elements of the traditional cinema experience by offering narrative, something to attract viewers who enter a room, sit in (semi)darkness, and become absorbed in a story. Yet the installation departs from the experience of cinema in its multiplication of stories and screens. *Widows* invites us to compare and contrast fourteen different narratives, fifteen screens, and two different formats (35mm and digital video). Moreover, the installation requires both movement and stasis on the part of the viewer. The viewer must change seats at least fourteen times in order to hear each widow's story. Viewers have the freedom to chart their own path through the widows' stories but must take into account the trajectories of others, and often wait for a chair to become available. There is no correct order to the stories. We listen to the widows in the order that circumstances allow, or according to those images that beckon us more strongly than others, which is both dependent upon the number of other viewers in the room and the moment and manner in which particular images strike us. We can choose to listen to all the stories, some of the stories, or none of the stories. This mixture of freedom, constraint, stasis, and movement in the viewing of multiple narratives on multiple screens draws on Varda's storytelling skills from her work in narrative cinema—the narratives told by the women are genuinely absorbing—but also reveals her understanding of the possibilities that the apparatus of an installation offers the artist.

The critical response to *L'île et elle* was resoundingly positive. Dominique Païni, former director of the Cinémathèque française and former curator at the Centre Pompidou, celebrated the heterogeneity of Varda's work: "Luckily Agnès V. scrutinizes and meddles in everything, experiments (a key word for this curious and cheeky woman) with, accentuates, borrows, and transforms everything. Theater photography, documentary, reportage, the cinematic essay, the filmed confession, unexpected fictions like *Le Bonheur*, filmed photography, the DVD boxed set with its supplements conceived as an artist's object" (34). Film and art critics alike thought it perfectly logical that Varda, the inveterate experimenter, would move into the realm of installations.

It must be said, however, that Varda did not sit passively by, hoping for a positive critical response to her installations. In addition to creating a catalogue for the exhibition, she actively shaped the response to her installations by commissioning essays on each work in the exhibition from important critics, journalists, and curators. The essays were published shortly after the opening of the exhibition in a volume titled *Regards sur l'exposition / Viewpoints on the Exhibition*.[22] Film theorist Raymond Bellour wrote about *Le Passage du Gois* while the writer and journalist Laure Adler contributed an affectionate tribute to *La Grande Carte postale ou Souvenir de Noirmoutier*. Actor Michel Piccoli wrote a poem about Varda and the island of Noirmoutier, while Museum of Modern Art curator Laurence Kardish contributed an essay about *Le Tombeau de Zgougou*.

With *L'île et elle*, Varda had pulled off a miraculous coup, bringing Noirmoutier back to her corner of the 14th arrondissement, finding the perfect balance of independent work at home and extended field research and interaction with locals on the ground in Vendée. Both *Patatutopia* and *L'île* gave Varda access to a new cultural marketplace, one in which she seems to have immersed herself: that of international art fairs, museums, and galleries. Her new work even allowed her to intervene in the politicocultural realm. In 2007, French president Jacques Chirac commissioned Varda to create an installation to be exhibited at the Pantheon in Paris titled *Les Justes (The Righteous)*, a work designed to honor the French who provided aid to Jews during World War II. In 2009, Varda unveiled another major suite of installations, this time in Sète, titled *La Mer . . . etSETEra (The Sea . . . etSETEra)*. In 2012, Varda created new installations for an exhibition at the Art Museum of the Central Academy of Fine Arts (CAFA) in Beijing, and in 2013 she unveiled an exhibition of installations and photographs entitled *Varda in Californialand* at the Los Angeles County Museum of Art. Varda succeeded not only in inserting herself credibly in this milieu, she put herself, both visually and spiritually, inside her work. She is both at its center and on the fringes, expanding on a persona she had cultivated in *Gleaners* and allowing it to build and reflect in much of her installation work, so much so that it (and the work of those installations) were refracted back into her subsequent work on film, as we shall see.

Looking Backward, Moving Forward:
The Beaches of Agnès

Les Plages d'Agnès (The Beaches of Agnès, 2008) is likely to be the culmination of Varda's life in the cinema (she has said as much, but it is too soon to count her out, obviously), offering a dizzying array of extracts and stills from her long career. But the film also reveals the impact of Varda's new profile as a plasticienne (visual artist). In the past decade, Varda's impact has spread from independent filmmaking to the most rarefied realm of the international fine arts scene. Now in her mid-eighties, her creative energy and cultural visibility undiminished, Varda continues to make installation art and is deeply engaged in the digital restoration of her work and the work of Jacques Demy. Her most recent documentary was a five-part series about contemporary art, Agnès de ci de là Varda (Agnès Varda Here and There, 2011).

Varda's work from 2000 to 2011, her sixth decade of art making, is marked by her ongoing commitment to certain strategies and values developed early on in her career, including above all the maintenance of artistic control over her work. In The Beaches, Varda's old friend from Los Angeles, producer Gerry Ayres, playfully reminds her that she could have made a film for Columbia Pictures in the late 1960s if only she had agreed to relinquish final cut.[23] Her work, however, the critical and commercial successes as well as the "flops," is emphatically her own. Although she regularly seeks friends' opinions on her rough cuts and once solicited the views of strangers via ciné-club surveys in the 1950s and the 1960s, Varda has never submitted to a higher authority on the final look or sound of her films. As of 2015, Varda's production company, Ciné-Tamaris, is still in operation on the rue Daguerre in the 14th arrondissement of Paris. Varda employs a small team that includes an editor, sales agent, graphic designer, archivist, administrative assistant, accountant, and the artist Julia Fabry, who works closely with Varda on the installations. Increasingly, Varda's children, Rosalie and Mathieu, have worked closely with her on the restoration of her and Demy's films.

In addition to retaining her basic business strategies running a small, independent production company that makes low-budget art films, documentaries, and installations funded through a mixture of public and private sources, Varda has retained several of her long-standing aesthetic strategies. These include, above all, the mixing of codes from fiction and documentary as well as her interest in conveying the specificity of place. Varda's documentaries over the past decade have intensified her use of travel and the resulting proliferation of locations. Whereas her early documentaries resemble travelogues, her later works, notably the fiction films *One Sings, the Other Doesn't* and *Vagabond*, feature protagonists who travel extensively and thus generate a "road film" structure. Her films from the past decade, *The Gleaners and I*, *The Beaches*, and *Agnès Varda Here and There* are structured explicitly around Varda's travels and the fortuitous encounters they engendered. Regardless of whether Varda draws upon the travelogue or the road film, her films continue to emphasize the specificity of "place" and to introduce an array of intriguing and often marginalized people. They also continue to offer a productive tension between a central organizational structure and elements of playful digression. Finally, Varda has retained her interest in the representation of time, sometimes manifested as a commitment to realist duration and sometimes to modernist kaleidoscope. As we have also seen, shooting and editing *The Gleaners and I* digitally afforded Varda many advantages: a low budget, an expanded shooting schedule, close contact with her subjects, and ease in editing a digressive, heterogeneous, fast-moving film. Both *The Beaches* and *Agnès Varda Here and There* adopt and extend many of these strategies.[24] *The Beaches* adds something new, however, to Varda's filmography: the unabashedly autobiographical work.

For the catalogue of *L'île et elle*, Varda had invited artist/animator/set designer Christophe Vallaux to sketch several caricatured images of herself, expanding on the playful and self-deprecating ways she had figured in *Patatutopia*. Vallaux created one image in particular that shows a diminutive, plump Varda perched on a comically high wooden chair, seemingly stranded in the low tide, presumably at Noirmoutier. The text below is captioned "Beacons and Lighthouses of France" as though from a coffee-table tome of coastal landmarks. The text reads: "Notable

A caricature of Varda by Christophe Vallaux
for the poster for *The Beaches of Agnès*.
© Ciné-Tamaris

for her cylindrical tower in trapezoidal form with exposed siding and small bags, crowned with red glasses, all on a fragile foundation sporting fabulous Chinese sandals. She remains an outstanding example of maritime architecture remotely operated from the rue Daguerre, currently without caretakers, she is however completely unsupervised and may not be visited."

The poster for *The Beaches* again called on Vallaux, expanding on this lovable, Magoo-like caricature and placing her this time on a very high director's chair. Vallaux's affectionate sketches bear witness to just how recognizable and consistent Varda's image—the Varda "look"—has been over the years. She has gradually evolved from an elfin *gamine* of the *Nouvelle Vague* to the punk granny of independent film and installation art. Her signature bowl-cut-cum-bob still frames her intelligent, impish face, although depending on the season and her humor, it can be fully aubergine or half grown-out into a two-toned monk's tonsorial fringe with a silvery cap. Her diminutive stature allows the caricaturist to exaggerate her into a plump butterball, but a 2009 photo of actress Tilda Swinton bending down to kiss Varda on the red carpet at the Cannes Festival is every bit as startling and amusing as Vallaux's endearing cartoons. If Varda's appearance seems both *negligée* and fastidiously *soignée*, it is emblematic of a paradox in her work: she has deliberately cultivated a down-to-earth persona through years of quietly observant self-portraiture and sympathetic identification with marginal figures, while placing herself resolutely in the center of that work with the narcissism of an irrepressible artist who must express herself or die. Invitations to participate in biennales and other fine arts exhibitions have reinforced the sense that Varda herself is the brand that is being sought out, and she has played along, offering further declensions of a playful, self-deprecating artist who wants to show us something. There is an urgency about what she wants to show us, however, just behind the humorous guise, and that urgency is the fervent belief that what Varda is looking at, what she has spotted, is of true and rare worth, deserving of our full attention. Varda is willing to clown a bit, but not at the expense of the dignity of her subjects or her attachment to the past. Varda's gift throughout her career, in the most fundamental sense, has been to make us take a look, and then a second look, and to oblige our skeptical eyes to "take an interest." This is made abundantly clear in her last film to date.

The Beaches of Agnès is, in one sense, a chronicle of the remarkable life of Agnès Varda. In roughly chronological fashion, we learn about her girlhood and adolescence, her education, her sexual coming of age, and her work as a photographer, a film director, and an installation artist. Her account of her life with Jacques Demy includes how she met him, their early years together, their separation in the early 1980s, their reunion in the late 1980s, and his death in 1990. Near the end, there is an oneiric, dance-like scene featuring Varda with her children and grandchildren on the beach in Noirmoutier, confirming the centrality of her immediate family in Varda's life. Chronicling the beaches that have marked her life also provides Varda's film with a structure based on geography, a go-to strategy for the filmmaker. This tactic allows Varda to inject the visual variety of multiple locations offered by the road film once again, taking her viewers from the beaches of her native Belgium to Sète, where she and her family lived on a boat during the war; to the island of Noirmoutier, where she and Demy spent their summers; and to Los Angeles, where she lived with Demy in the late 1960s and without him in 1979–80. Varda even manages to reimagine her beloved rue Daguerre in the middle of Paris as a beach, thanks to a few tons of sand and the approval of the mayor's office.

Despite the film's apparent devotion to chronology and its clearly marked geographical framework, *The Beaches* is a highly unusual autobiography. The film's temporal structure is actually quite loose; Varda's narration moves back and forth through time in unpredictable ways. Likewise, Varda's film extracts and stills do not always correspond to the period being recounted in Varda's life. This intention to move freely through time is articulated clearly in an early scenario for the film: "We will see in the Sète episode photographs of several [theatrical] productions even if I became a photographer later" (Varda, Ciné-Tamaris, *Les Plages d'Agnès*, 9). Moreover, for an autobiography, the film concentrates very little on the details of Varda's childhood; in fact, in one early scene, she flatly denies that her childhood inspired her in any way or could provide the key to the person she became. The film instead focuses most insistently on creating a tapestry of Varda's work, incorporating a huge number of still and moving images from her long career into her life story.[25]

One of the film's most startling strategies is its use of re-enactment. Varda stages scenes from the past as well as fantasies from the present with extraordinary variety and invention. The film's precredit sequence, for example, shows Varda with her assistants creating a complex installation on a beach in Belgium involving the anchoring of mirrors in the sand. The scene provides an idea of how Varda works with her assistants (quickly and with confidence, authority, and humor) and how, precisely, she goes about executing an installation. The mirrors have both literal and conceptual functions, conjuring up Varda's memories about the mirrored armoire in her parents' room, for example, but also serving as an apt metaphor for the autobiographical story she is about to tell. Mirrors,

Varda at work in the prologue of
The *Beaches of Agnès* (2008). © Ciné-Tamaris

like all autobiographies, sometimes reflect people and landscapes with reasonable fidelity, yet can also fragment and distort.

Varda's reflection on the inevitably fragmentary nature of autobiography is articulated even more directly in the scene in Avignon in which she prepares an exhibition of her photographs of actors from the Théâtre National Populaire taken in the 1950s. One of the photographs, of actor Gérard Philipe, is a huge image that she has divided into several parts, an act that prompts her to muse about fragmentation and to ask, "Is reconstruction possible?" Such scenes emphasize the film's "fragmented, multiple and de-centered representations" of Varda herself (Bluher 59–69).

It quickly becomes apparent that Varda is less interested in excavating some definitive, coherent version of herself from the past than she is in engaging in the creation of new work, a series of highly stylized, installation-like scenes that represent her memories or fantasies. Varda mentions this specifically in the screenplay for *The Beaches*: "It is the goal of this film to try to incorporate Agnès' memories in the framework of her current activity." Such scenes possess a variety of connections to her films and her life history, and they are rarely simple. For example, to narrate her family's move from Sète to Paris in 1944, we see several shots of Varda (c. 2008) navigating a boat through the canals of Sète. Still in a boat, she passes by La Pointe Courte and mentions in voice-over that she named her first film after this neighborhood. We then see an extract from *La Pointe Courte*, the last shot of the film, which features a boat similar to the one Varda navigates slicing through the water. We see the boat from behind as it moves from the foreground to the background of the shot. In the background, a train moves laterally, from left to right, transporting the squabbling couple from *La Pointe Courte* back to Paris. Next, a graphic match connects this shot with the subsequent shot: present-day Varda navigating a boat on the Seine in Paris, moving from foreground to the background of the frame. A train enters the background frame left, suggesting that this shot is a continuation of the final shot of her 1955 film. The scene does not exactly re-enact something that happened in Varda's past, although she did learn how to sail as an adolescent in Sète. Rather, the scene is a witty and elegant transition from one part of Varda's life to the next as well as an imaginary extension of the final shot of her first film. The scene is thus anything but a simple transition from one chapter of her life to the next; it illustrates

Varda navigating the Seine in
The *Beaches of Agnès* (2008). © Ciné-Tamaris

her family's 1944 move from Sète to Paris using both the final shot of a film she would shoot in 1954 and footage shot in both Sète and Paris in 2008.[26] Another staged scene, the trapeze performance, is neither a reconstructed memory nor an extension of one of her films, but rather the realization of a fantasy Varda had while a young girl. Her voice-over tells us, "As a teenager, I'd dream of joining a circus. . . . I knew nothing of life." The film's brisk editing pace slows momentarily so the troop can perform its show. Varda films the performance from a high angle against the backdrop of the sea, using both still and moving images. Varda then humorously inserts herself into her own fantasy by posing with the trapeze artists for the camera while dressed in a red satin costume. The gorgeous physicality of the trapeze performance culminates in the embrace of an unidentified nude couple lying in the sand, which affords Varda the chance to introduce the topic of sex into her narrative, something she handles with particular wit in the film. The fantasy sequences often function to halt the documentary's narrative, departing momentarily from the basic chronology of Varda's life, but above all they allow her to experiment with digitally layered compositions, with stillness combined with movement and with vibrant color in costume and décor.

Crucially, Varda never tries to obscure the staged nature of such scenes, unlike, for example, Sarah Polley's *Stories We Tell* (2012), an autobiographical film that strategically conceals the staged status of approximately half of its lovingly re-enacted "home movie" footage until late in the film. Instead, Varda foregrounds the performative nature of the act of telling one's life story. She accomplishes this by simply speaking directly to the camera, but more often through the staging of a scene from the past or the re-enactment of a fantasy. She uses many avatars to represent herself at different stages of her life, including the little girls on the beach, the singing schoolgirl in her gingham pinafore in Sète, the twenty-year-old who mends a fishing net in Corsica and later writes the screenplay for *La Pointe Courte* in the garden courtyard on rue Daguerre. Again and again, we are made to feel Varda's exhilaration in departing from a strictly chronological, evidence-based account of her life. The repeated gesture of walking backward on a beach exemplifies this performative, playful impulse; walking backward is meant to indicate Varda's numerous journeys "back in time," but she actually moves freely both backward and forward, and from memory to fantasy, in vertiginous, propulsive fashion. Such techniques move *The Beaches* away from the traditional expository or observational documentary and closer to a film such as *My Winnipeg* (2007), Guy Maddin's wry autobiographical documentary that combines archival footage with staged footage to evoke his family history and hometown.

The Beaches was initially born of Varda's dawning awareness that she would soon turn eighty and that she would like to recount her memories for her grandchildren and for young audiences who only knew *The Gleaners and I.* She wanted to find an "amusing and inventive" way to "recount an artist's life as an ordinary life (Domenach and Rouyer 17). People she did not know well had approached her with the idea of making a biographical documentary about her, but that prospect did not appeal to her (Varda, *Les plages d'Agnès*, promotional pamphlet, 3). Initially reluctant to make an autobiographical film, Varda considered having Didier Rouget, her assistant director since the making of *Jacquot de Nantes*, create a biographical film about her. The first step in making the film entailed the shooting of the mirror scene on the Belgian beach with Rouget in the role of codirector. The experience was positive, but Varda decided to move forward as the sole director and writer of the film, using the Belgium scene as a "sizzle reel" to raise funds.

By July 2007, Varda had written the first draft of the screenplay for the film. This time, in contrast to the more rudimentary scrapbook photo album she created for her documentary *L'Opéra-Mouffe* or the prose descriptions and lists of possible scenes for *Gleaners*, Varda produced a document that used both prose and images and possessed a clear structure and considerable detail. She organized the document around the five beaches that have marked her life: the North Sea beaches in Belgium, the Mediterranean beaches of Sète, the Pacific Ocean in Los Angeles, the Atlantic Ocean in Noirmoutier, and the ersatz beach she created on the street in front of her home base in Paris. Each section of the screenplay begins with a collage featuring photocopied postcards, film stills, and family photographs. The screenplay indicates the texts to be read in voice-over by Varda, lists the many film clips Varda anticipated using, and describes in some detail many of the reconstituted scenes.

The five sections are further divided into subsections. The chapter of the scenario devoted to Belgium, for example is subdivided into: (1) "the installation of mirrors near the sea," (2) "Arlette [Varda's original first name] as a child, swimsuits, flowers and shells," (3) "In search of the past (which one? Before? After?)," (4) "My House or that of a collector?" and (5) "The universe of images and vignettes." The screenplay occasionally provides scenes that did not make it into the final cut of the film and occasionally omits scenes that were created later. For example, the two versions of the screenplay do not mention the trapeze performance on the beach in Sète. In place of the trapeze sequence, the screenplays contain a scene in which Varda erects a monument to her mother made up of objects her mother loved.

Varda had in fact already shot and edited a significant portion of the film before creating the first draft of the screenplay. This document is thus a record of what she had already completed for the film *and* a plan for what she anticipates doing next. It is also, crucially, a fundraising tool for the production, one that was sent to Arte, Canal+, and other funding sources. As a result, there is a self-consciousness about this document and an attempt to persuade the reader of the future film's power. There is even a kind of user's manual, a section titled "A Note for the Reader of the Scenario," at the beginning: "The scenario that follows is rather a work plan, a method for filming, a canvas indicating places and trajectories, the themes of my subject, some staging and editing choices and some plans for reenacted scenes." The sections on Belgium and Sète are, naturally, more detailed than the section on Los Angeles, which was shot later. Varda acknowledges some uncertainty, stating, "I already wrote some voiceover commentaries and some possible conversations but it is impossible to anticipate what I will say to my interlocutors."

There is yet another portion of the scenario that foregrounds Varda's intentions at the end of the document. This is a second, much longer, explanatory note titled "Note de présentation et d'intention" ("Note of Presentation and Intention"). This text repeats some of the information from the brief "note to the reader" at the front; it again explains the "beach" structure but also emphasizes her incorporation of clips. "This project is to recount myself, as a woman and as a filmmaker, by my current activities and recent projects, but especially through the images of my films and my installations: a biographical film [*bio-film*] as a pretext for a filmography-film [*filmo-film*]." The film will be, above all, a tapestry of film clips that tells the life story of Varda. *The Beaches*, the document indicates, will also be innovative as a documentary by signaling authenticity as well as using techniques associated with fiction: "I hope to innovate in making a 'self-documentary' that is fluid and entertaining but fractured into an incomplete story, between sincerity and representation."

Varda used another conceptual tool in planning *The Beaches*: the database. In many interviews, she states that she thought of her entire filmography as a vast database she could use in her autobiographical film. Accordingly, she accesses her "database" of clips with great liberty and agility to narrate her professional and personal trajectory. Such a conception leads to a heterogeneous, fractured film, edited with careful attention to graphic matches and associative logic. This accumulation of conceptual tools in the planning of Varda's films, from the photo album-notebook used in the preparation of *L'Opéra-Mouffe* to the "database" of *Les Plages d'Agnès*, reflects in part the availability of digital tools.

Varda continued to use the nonlinear working method she had employed while making her first digital work, *The Gleaners and I*, interweaving the processes of writing, shooting, and editing. Varda had already begun interweaving the editing phase with the shooting phase during the making of *Vagabond*, but digital editing had since afforded her even more freedom to mix the different phases of production. Her standard working method now involved the interspersion of reflection, writing, traveling, shooting, the recording of the voice-over, editing, and the shooting of still more material. Varda is not alone in having adopted such working methods. As Millard notes, "Acclaimed writers and filmmakers, including Gus Van Sant, Jim Jarmusch, Tony Grisoni, Michael Winterbottom, Wong Kar Wai, Wim Wenders and Chantal Akerman, have all developed methods of shifting between writing and production, working with both words and images" ("After the Typewriter," 13).

The shooting period for *The Beaches* lasted nearly two years, from August 2006 to June 2008, much longer than the nine-month intermittent shoot of *Gleaners* (Varda, *Les plages d'Agnès*, promotional pamphlet). The scenes in Belgium were shot in June 2006, shortly after *L'île et elle* opened at the Cartier Foundation, but most of the film's shooting took place in 2007 (Domenach and Rouyer 21). Varda's working rhythm can be intuited from her 2007 schedule. An initial, detailed draft of the scenario was completed by July 16, 2007. She shot the Avignon scene in July 2007 and the Sète scenes in August 2007. A second draft of the screenplay was completed in November 2007. Varda shot the Los Angeles scenes in November 2007 and shot in Paris "all the time" (Domenach and Rouyer 21). She worked with her editors intermittently throughout 2007, but starting in January 2008 she engaged in intensive editing and mixing until the end of August in an attempt to be able to show the finished film at the Venice Film Festival (Domenach and Rouyer 21). As with *Gleaners*, she shot lots of material and opted for a digressive, discontinuous film whose aesthetic achievement is heavily reliant upon associative editing.

While shooting *The Beaches* took two years, the editing went on during one and a half of those years. Varda worked with two editors during the making of the film, her long-time editor Jean-Baptiste Morin and Baptiste Filloux. "They accepted my method, they know that I write or *ciné*-write the film during editing, and that it takes a long time. We had so much material for *The Beaches* we rented a second editing station, and the two editors worked all the time. I went from one to the other. On one side was Sète and Los Angeles, in the other room was Belgium and Paris" (Domenach and Rouyer 21).

One of her challenges was to find the right tonal balance: "I reflected, I wrote my commentary, I tried it out loud, and then we changed the montage. Then I went into the other room. What took so much time in the editing was finding the right equilibrium, or a kind of equilibrium, between the story, modesty and emotion" (Domenach and Rouyer 21). When Varda had to leave Paris to present a film or install an exhibition, she left ideas on paper for the editors so the editors could continue working without her.

The film was shown in late August 2008 at the Venice Film Festival and in early September at the Toronto International Film Festival, where it enjoyed a positive reception. But after those festivals, Varda returned to her editing room in Paris once again to further tighten the film, a time-consuming and expensive process even with digital video, since it required remixing the sound and redoing the color grading. As Varda tightened up the film in the editing room, she created a more somber tone, moving away from humor. "I had less desire to show myself in my potato costume, to wear my rabbit fur boots and to play the clown. It's the trajectory of the film that demanded that. Little by little, one takes one's distance from youth. One arrives at an age in which meditation, the understanding of others and tears take up more space. The film evolved like real life" (Domenach and Rouyer).

The budget for *The Beaches* was 1.9 million euros (approximately US$2.5 million) (Rose). This is high for a European documentary, but low compared to the average cost of a French fiction film in 2008, which was 5.4 million euros (US$7 million) (European Audiovisual Observatory).[27] The majority of the budget for *The Beaches* came from Ciné-Tamaris, while modest subsidies came from Arte, Canal+, the administrative regions Ile-de-France and Languedoc Roussillon, and a CNC "Innovation" grant (Rose).

The film enjoyed a positive critical reception and respectable performance at the box office. Whereas *Gleaners* had attracted 120,000 viewers in France, *The Beaches* attracted 239,761 viewers in France and many more in festivals and art cinemas in other countries. The film was distributed theatrically in France, Belgium, the Netherlands, Brazil, Argentina, Portugal, Japan, the UK, Luxembourg, Korea, Canada, and the United States. *The Beaches* won a César for Best Documentary, was designated "Best Film" by the French Syndicate of Cinema Critics, and won "Best Documentary" awards from the Directors Guild of America, the Los Angeles Film Critics Association, and the National Society of Film Critics.

Conclusion

The process of creating *The Beaches of Agnès* understandably caused Varda to reflect on how she has spent her life. In a recent interview, she acknowledged that one of the things that became apparent to her was how *much* she had worked (Domenach and Rouyer). Essentially, she realized, she has never stopped working. In between the making of her feature films she has always made short films. Since 2003, between making three major documentaries (two features and the television series), she has never ceased making installation art and exhibiting it in museums around the world. The exhibition of her work has always been an important part of the filmmaking process for Varda. In the same reflective interview, Varda expressed surprise at how much time she has spent over the years "accompanying" her films to festivals and retrospectives. She reiterated her belief in the importance of talking about her work with viewers, not so much to enhance profits, but because "[t]he impressions of those who have seen my work nourish me and make me reflect. Sometimes that irritates me. What am I transmitting about the world? How do people perceive it? Imagining the perception of a film by others is truly our métier. More than making exceptional films" (Domenach and Rouyer 19). Imagining the perception of a film by others, establishing connections with people, are in the end the most important to Varda.

In the course of such a long career, a few aesthetic dead ends are inevitable. Varda made a science fiction film, *The Creatures* (1965), that flopped at the box office, and she never ventured in that direction again, except to recycle 35mm prints of the film for her installation *My Failure Shack* (2006). In 1958 she made an apparently malicious documentary about kept women on the Riviera, *Les Cocottes de la côte*, but chose not to release it and has removed it from her filmography. While living in Los Angeles in the late 1960s, a period of her career that deserves more attention than I can give it here, Varda made *Lions Love*, a film inspired by the experimental cinema of Andy Warhol and featuring his muse, Viva. But she never revisited that work's particular combination of long takes, improvised direct address, and use of television footage. Also while in Los Angeles, she made a documentary titled *Black Panthers* (1968) in an expository style that bears little trace of the reflexivity and performative quality of her other documentaries.

And yet my study has revealed more continuity than creative ruptures in Varda's working methods and aesthetics over the years. First, Varda's insistence upon total artistic control over her work is a constant. She has always created original screenplays for her films, has never codirected a film, and has always controlled the final cut of her work. Even in the rare cases when others have provided the topics for her films, such as the commissioned documentaries made in the late 1950s, her work has been stamped with a distinctive point of view and aesthetic. Varda still uses the term she coined decades ago, *cinécriture* (cine-writing), to evoke the wide range of aesthetic decisions she makes during the course of each and every project.

Careful planning and extensive scouting have always been part of her working method, but over time, Varda has engaged in increasing levels of improvisation during the shoots themselves. The avatar Varda conjures in *The Beaches* of the young woman writing every line of the screenplay for *La Pointe Courte* in her courtyard every Sunday has given way to an updated Varda, creating on the fly, incessantly on the move, filming on the road in *The Gleaners* and on transatlantic planes in *Agnès Varda Here and There*, responding to unforeseen stimuli or serendipitous mishaps.

Digital technology has, in one sense, allowed Varda to do more easily what she has always done with 35mm or 16mm film. While shooting *Vagabond*, Varda was already mixing the task of editing with principal photography, but digital tools have allowed her to interweave even more extensively the stages of writing, shooting, and editing. Varda has always created unconventional characters in her fiction films and has always sought out marginalized or uncommon people for her documentary films, but the small digital camera has increased her access to her subjects, from the homeless people of *The Gleaners* to the grieving widows of Noirmoutier, herself included. Varda has long conveyed the specificity of place, but her geographical range has expanded enormously through the years, from the focus on one neighborhood in the town of Sète to her far-flung friends in Los Angeles (in *The Beaches of Agnès*) to the international community of artists and curators in *Agnès Varda Here and There*. And yet it comes to rest, as all her journeys do, back in the 14th arrondissement, where she is equally at home reinventing Noirmoutier at the Cartier Foundation or reconstructing a beach on the rue Daguerre.

Varda's work has continued to manifest an aesthetic commitment to realism and to formal rigor as well as to the melding of fiction and documentary. Her work since 2000 extends her career-long tendency to try new aesthetic strategies, many of them refined from her installation work, notably the intensification of associative editing, the layering of images using digital tools, the use of collage techniques, and experimentation with the proliferation of screens. Varda's willingness to put herself front and center in her work has also intensified since 2000. *The Gleaners and I, The Beaches of Agnès*, and *The Widows of Noirmoutier* challenge traditional autobiographical strategies by configuring memory as unstable and by privileging staging over more traditional documentary techniques.

Varda's trajectory as an artist should not be considered apart from the contextual factors that have shaped it. The postwar French effort to democratize culture through institutions such as the TNP and the *ciné-club* positively affected Varda's professional life and aesthetic commitments, as did the rise of European art cinema, the *Nouvelle Vague*, and the international film festival. Also affecting Varda's work and her conception of herself were myriad political developments, notably feminism, which I have only touched on briefly. Perhaps it is because of my strong conviction that certain aspects of Varda's work, while nourished by developments in film culture and the sociopolitical realm, ultimately resist contextual explanation. One such element is Varda's incessant desire to create and her capacity to build on her past work without repeating herself. Julia Fabry, Varda's assistant since *The Beaches*, isolates something crucial, I believe, when she observes that Varda tends to work and live in the moment, willing to reflect on the past but only when it serves a current creative project.[28]

And this begins to drive at the most crucial continuity in Varda's work: her ability to read narrative in provocative, often desolate landscapes, in the faces of marginal figures seemingly in the background but no less vital or primary for that reason, on multiple planes and in multiple times and rhythms of durations. This skill, or passion, or driving motivation, whatever one chooses to call it, has allowed Varda to conceive and operate in the multiple rooms of the art gallery, adapting her storytelling to fill huge polyvalent spaces and manipulate viewers through the plastic realm of her imagination, which is given shape, brought to life, or cobbled, recycled, and reconstructed from found objects, recovered footage, and reimagined memories. Conversely, this explosion of the flat cinematic plane into the space of the gallery has allowed her to refine her cinematic vision and strategies from the improvisations of *Vagabond* to the investigations and formal play of *Gleaners*, and from there to "Potatoland" and "Island" and even "Californialand," to their culmination in her summational journey in *The Beaches*.

* * *

Although it had long been on my wish list since seeing Varda's installations at the Cartier Foundation, I'd never personally visited Noirmoutier. Between trying to finalize research in Paris in June of 2012 and attempting to pin an elusive Varda down for the interview she'd promised that would round out this volume, it wasn't a priority. Varda was away from Paris overseeing a new pair of installations in Nantes, her late husband's childhood home, which made it doubly difficult. I weighed the advantages of making my way to Vendée, knowing Varda would be fully occupied with launching the exhibit. These installations had been commissioned by the city as part of a show, *Voyages à Nantes* (*Journeys to Nantes*), the name evoking the myriad narratives that may have been launched from the busy river port near the mouth of Loire, which opens into the Atlantic just south of Brittany. Should I undertake a journey myself, if only to see the exhibition before I left France? While there, I could try to urge Varda to commit to a date for the interview. My plan was to head out and back to Paris in a single day, but when I ran into Varda at the installations, she invited me to the spend the weekend at the Noirmoutier millhouse she and Demy had restored. I couldn't say no.

The two installations in question, *Des Chambres en ville* (*Rooms in Town*) and *La Chambre occupée* (*The Occupied Room*), exemplify perfectly the unique exchange Varda transacted between stories narrated on screen and those gleaned from life between the formal shape and constraints of a film, and how that can yet be molded and refined by the space of the gallery. Both installations were, not surprisingly, an homage to Jacques Demy, drawing inspiration from one of his later films, *Une Chambre en ville* (*A Room in Town*, 1982), with Michel Piccoli, Dominique Sanda, and Richard Berry. The set of the television shop managed by Michel Piccoli's character was recreated in Varda's installation, which consisted of three parts. The first part was a bank of six television screens, three on top and three on the bottom, transmitting contrasting types of footage. On the top row, screens displayed images Varda took in the Passage Pomeraye (made famous in Demy's *Lola*) of passersby. The bottom row featured two screens showing historical footage of barges and workers in the port and a third screen with images of anonymous people voting in the city in a recent legislative election.

Seen at their most basic level, the screens documented public spaces in Nantes, past and present. In the editing of the video images taken in the Passage Pomeraye, Varda drew upon a technique she used in *Noirmoutier Triptych* in which adjacent screens are configured as both off-screen and on-screen space. For example, a passerby would cross through the frame, exit, and then reappear on the adjacent screen in continuity of sequence. This room also contained a television set on the opposite side of the wall broadcasting a live feed.

By pure chance, a report on Jacques Demy was showing on that feed and Varda was in the room, sorting out some minor technical issues. The television was experiencing transmission problems as the image kept breaking up and dissolving. Varda watched in irritation at first, exhorting one of the docents to find a technician to fix the problem immediately, but she soon became fascinated by the decomposition of Demy's face; he would appear, then fade out, then reappear, all to bizarrely beautiful effect, eerily, as if a medium were trying with great difficulty to call up the spirit of the late director. Varda's improvisational instincts took over, her characteristic flexibility in the artistic process seizing upon something good when it came along, and she gleefully set about filming the television screen with her video camera. A second component of the installation was an adjacent room in which extracts from Demy's film were looped on a large screen. Notably, an especially gruesome scene in which Piccoli draws a razor across his throat, the blood spurting all over Dominique Sanda, was shown repeatedly. Finally, a third setup comprised a workroom in the back of the "shop" where spare television parts were stored, along with a fur coat similar to the one worn by Dominique Sanda in the film.

The second installation, *La Chambre occupée*, revealed similar links, both political and social, with the project of Varda's *Gleaners*. The work, which addressed the experience of squatters in France, was set upstairs in that same Passage Pomeraye, a merchant arcade, in what appeared to be abandoned apartments. There were three screens embedded in domestic objects: a microwave, a mattress propped upright, and an old-fashioned stove. On the television screens were loops of images in which squatters, mostly black and all obviously marginalized, speak about their experiences of being evicted from their living spaces. There was an audio component to the installation. Upon entering, one heard muffled voices, as if the occupants of adjacent apartments were talking. The installation was both emotionally moving and politically charged. The idea of embedding screens in domestic spaces in an unexpected way recalled Godard's evocative 2006 exhibition at Beaubourg, in which he placed flat-screen televisions on a kitchen table (projecting porn in the kitchen), in the bedroom (screening Ridley Scott's *Blackhawk Down*, 2001) and in the living room (Bernard Borderie's *La Môme vert-de-gris / Poison Ivy*, 1952). But Varda's mise-en-scene of the screens asked the viewer to think more directly about a pressing political issue: social inequality, homelessness, and the precariousness of the lives of undocumented immigrants. The political component was clear, while the apparatus as a whole was appealingly intricate and even witty. (The video in the microwave rotated as if it were food being reheated.) There was also a smashed mirror in the room similar to those used in *Portraits brisées*, photographs taken by Varda in which human faces appear fragmented or cracked. Finally, the installation also featured a wall posted with news articles about housing problems and legal information about squatting. As noted previously, I had traced some of the inspiration for this installation to our 2005 breakfast together in Montreal, when Varda was captivated by the sight of several homeless people outside our hotel and began speculating about their stories. But it also owed much to her work on *Gleaners*, both in its political concerns touching upon privation and shelter (thus, too, harking back to *Vagabond*), but also in its material gleaning, as if Varda had rummaged around the actual sets of Demy's film, pillaging and plundering its décor for the bits and pieces of her installation, yet clearly also scavenging junk heaps to recreate the very décor from which she appears to have gleaned the installation. It is a dizzying *mise-en-abîme*, the continual gleaning that makes up Varda's essential two-pronged technique of observing and *"cinécriture,"* and the mirrors cast back and forth, like those on her beaches, reflecting the filmwork into the gallery and then refracting the multiplicity of narratives contained or suggested by her installations, honed laser-like back into her filmwork.

* * *

On the road to Noirmoutier: Laura Gross, who first worked as an intern at Ciné-Tamaris and has now become a friend and valued research assistant on this project, drives us. There are a few wrong turns and dead ends before we finally reach the famous Passage du Gois, with its submersible stretch of road connecting the mainland to the island. We have timed it to avoid high tide, and have the uncanny sentiment that we are living inside Varda's installation from *L'île et elle*. We stop in town to catch our breath and to shop for postcards at a flea market that has been set up in a central square. I search the faces for any I may know: Are any of these women I encounter widows? Are they Varda's widows? We get back into the car after once more asking directions, and arrive *chez Agnès* with great relief. And to much fanfare; we scarcely have time to unload the car when we are herded back out to the market before it closes. Nowhere in the rest of France can you buy the range of fresh fish and seafood found in Vendée. We buy an appealing *merlan* or whiting and some *crevettes roses*, the small pink shrimp that are a regional delicacy. I make noises about conducting the interview before dinner, but Varda insists there will be plenty of time afterwards. She has also invited her friend Isabelle Cahen, Ciné-Tamaris's office manager in the 1980s, and the four of us prepare dinner. The whiting is exquisite, and Varda has also prepared her favorite *bonnotte* potatoes, a specialty of the island. I meekly bring up the interview again, but Varda proposes instead a game of Scrabble, which we play late into the night. Varda is hypercompetitive, a walking, breathing dictionary—unsurprising, given the prodigious wordplay on display throughout her work—and the rest of us don't stand a chance.

The next day, rested and energized by the island air and her latest installation efforts, magnanimous in victory (but mainly true to her word), she grants me the interview. In the kitchen of her Noirmoutier home, the same kitchen that serves as the set in *Triptych of Noirmoutier*, she speaks eloquently about her life and work for nearly two hours. I have never felt so intimately connected to the world and process I've been studying for nearly ten years. To temper my elation, I remind myself that Varda has several shelves of her library back on rue Daguerre that are devoted to the published scholarship on her films. She once confided to me that she had not yet found time to read many of them.

* * *

At the 2015 Cannes Film Festival Agnès Varda became the first woman and the first French director to be awarded the prestigious Palme d'honneur. In her acceptance speech, Varda gave a nod to the past, noting that her award would take up residence on rue Daguerre in the cabinet next to the Palme d'or won by Jacques Demy in 1964 (for *Umbrellas of Cherbourg*). Varda's past has certainly nourished her work, notably in the making of the documentaries about Demy in the early 1990s, in the installations steeped in references to her beloved Noirmoutier, and in the kaleidoscopic, clip-filled *Beaches of Agnès*. She has also looked to the past in her incessant and inventive recycling of objects, images, characters, or ideas from her own work. But Varda is, above all, an artist who moves forward, both in her day-to-day working methods and in her overall aesthetic trajectory, expanding her storytelling methods and stylistic experiments and seeking new audiences and new exhibition contexts. If the past is any indicator, Varda will continue to move forward in the years to come, drawing inventively on her previous work while seeking the new.

Notes

1. Bienvenida Llorca also appears in Varda's short film *Réponses des femmes*. Her son, Ulysse, would later be the subject of Varda's 1982 film *Ulysse*.
2. In the article, Bazin reported that Varda's *La Pointe Courte* had won the "Prix des Cinéphiles" created by Armand Cauliez and his ciné-club. Rossellini's *Journey to Italy* won the club's prize for best foreign film. Bazin, "Petit Journal Intime du cinéma."
3. For example, while Varda made *Du côté de la côte*, she also made another documentary with footage she shot at the same time: *La Cocotte d'Azur*. She was not happy with this film, ultimately, and withdrew it from circulation. See Bastide, "Agnès Varda," and Gorbman, "Finding a Voice," 40–57.
4. For a striking contrast to Varda's poetic approach to the rue Mouffetard, see the documentary *Rue Mouffetard* (Jacques Krier, 1959), which treats the neighborhood with a "social problem" approach. The film is made up of interviews of the shopkeepers and inhabitants, alarming statistics on the poor living conditions (in which we learn that the street contains 9,000 inhabitants and 4,000 apartments, only 2,500 of which have running water), and finally a roundtable discussion with sociologists filmed in a studio.
5. Sam Siritzky was the distributor of *Cleo from 5 to 7* as well as many other art house films.
6. Serge Daney's responses to the questionnaire are reprinted in Varda, *Varda par Agnès*, 236.
7. Michel Dancourt, "Cléo: 97% de Oui," *Arts* 865, April 18–24, 1962.
8. Bory, "Ce qu'il a de changé. Here Bory isolates the elements of "modern" cinema and cites *Cleo's* brief flashbacks, its natural décor and lighting, its lack of dramatic crane shots or "camera movement for the sake of it," and its story

that avoids the *"exposition, noeud, dénouement"* (exposition, knot, disentangling of the knot) in favor of ambiguity.

9. Sandy Flitterman-Lewis notes that the film's structure is a playful reworking of *Citizen Kane* in that it begins and ends with the death of a poor, young woman instead of a wealthy old man. See Flitterman-Lewis's authoritative narrative and feminist analysis of the film in *To Desire Differently*.

10. My account of *Vagabond*'s production history draws heavily upon documents found at the Ciné-Tamaris archive, notably a dossier titled "Comment j'ai imaginé, préparé et peu écrit avant de tourner *Sans toit ni loi*" (How I imagined, prepared, and wrote little before shooting *Vagabond*). A subtitle of this document clarifies that the document consists of "notes from 1986, one year after the film's release, completed in 1993." This material was gathered for a book Varda had planned to write on *Vagabond*, but the project did not come to fruition.

11. René Prédal's book on the film, *Sans toit ni loi d'Agnès Varda*, was in fact published in a collection designed to help students prepare for this exam.

12. For analyses of Varda's music, see Calatayus, Gorbman, "Varda's Music;" and Vesey.

13. In an article authored by Varda and published in *Les Inrockuptibles* six months after the release of *The Gleaners and I*, Varda specifically gives thanks for "tous les spectateurs qui me parlent ou m'écrivent, m'evoient des images, des coquillages, des récits, des fleurs et des mots d'amour" (all the viewers who talk to me or write to me, send me images, shells, stories, flowers, and words of love). Varda, "La moissonneuse-battante," 73.

14. Those who have had the good fortune to see Varda introduce her films in public or engage in a question-and-answer session after a screening know that she is particularly gifted at both analyzing her own work and establishing a dialogue with her viewers. Not all filmmakers are skilled at these types of exchanges. Varda's desire to hear what viewers think of her work is reflected early in her career in the *ciné-club* surveys she collected after the screenings of *La Pointe Courte* and *Cleo from 5 to 7*, while her pleasure in explaining her goals and intentions can be seen vividly in her DVD supplements, as well as in her career-long habit of accompanying her films to festivals and retrospectives.

15. Benoist, "Stéphane Krausz," 24–27. "(il y avait parfois une période d'un mois sans tournage), il est arrive qu'il ne soit pas libre car il travaille beaucoup, et qu'il réalise lui-même des films. Sur une heure vingt j'ai donc fait vingt minutes toute seule, sans Stéphane et sans les trois autres opérateurs."

16. The attendance figure of 120,000 comes from Diatkine and Lefort, "Varda, la glaneuse vagabonde."

17. See Varda's five-part documentary *Agnès de ci de là Varda* for footage of *Patatutopia* at a subsequent exhibition of the installation in Stockholm. Footage of the installation can also be seen in *The Beaches of Agnès* (2008).

18. As if aware of the potential criticism that her contribution to Utopia Station was excessively whimsical, Varda acknowledged in the Biennale catalogue

the risk of making art about the modest subject of the potato in a world of war, hunger, and death.

On the first days of April 2003, when we are asked to write 200 words for the program of the Biennale in June, the people of Baghdad are being bombed day and night. More than a million citizens of Bassora, including the wounded and the newborn, do not have access to drinkable water. Civilians are dying, as well as soldiers. In several parts of the world, refugees are walking on the roads and here we are (is it untimely? absurd? idiotic even?) thinking about utopias, talking about utopia and, as for myself, filming Patatutopia, a fancy-fair show made of images both real and dreamy, an homage to potatoes. I had the chance to encounter heart-shaped potatoes. I watched them and watched over them. They had got old and germinated again. Yes, I dare to evoke this utopia, a belief that the beauty of the world, as perceived in a potato skin or a potato sprout, helps us live and reconciles us with the world. My wish is that those who step into the 'potato shack' will be moved by and smile in front of the most common and modest of all vegetables, the potato (French nickname 'patate').

19. The cost of *Patatutopia* was less than five thousand euros, according to planning documents at Ciné-Tamaris.

20. Jean-Michel Frodon writes of the extraordinary increase of museum exhibitions that incorporate cinema in one way or another in "Cinémamusée: Le grand tournant, 8. The entire April 2006 issue of *Cahiers du cinéma* is devoted to the topic. See also the useful work of Erika Balsom, *Exhibiting Cinema in Contemporary Art*, and Steven Jacobs, *Framing Pictures: Film and the Visual Arts*.

21. For a more detailed description of each installation and the layout of the exhibition at the Fondation Cartier, see Conway, "The New Wave in the Museum," 195–217.

22. Varda, *Agnès Varda, L'île et elle*.

23. Ayres is referring to the unfinished project *Peace and Love*.

24. For information on Varda as a filmmaker working in the context of globalization and for an analysis of *Agnès Varda Here and There*, see Conway, "Responding to Globalization."

25. See my discussion of the heterogeneous array of material in *The Beaches of Agnès*, the film's structure and its associative editing, and the results of such choices on Varda's rhetorical project. Conway, "Varda at Work," 125–39.

26. The shot of Varda in a boat in Paris took six hours to shoot and involved the synchronization of two boats (one holding Varda, the other holding the director of photography) with the passing of the aerial metro train on the bridge. Varda had to avoid colliding with barges and boats on the river and also maintain the visibility of the Eiffel Tower. Email with author, Agnès Varda, May 4, 2014.

27. All these figures seem quite low, however, when one considers that the average budget of an American fiction film in 2008 was US$107 million.

28. Fabry, interview with author. "C'est vrai qu'elle a une personnalité qui est d'être dans une dynamique permanente, d'aller toujours de l'avant et de ne jamais regarder en arrière. Donc, si elle a fait des choses sur lesquelles elle s'est penchée sur son passé, c'est uniquement, pour, comme une matière dont elle se servirait pour sa création, mais c'est jamais, ça ne l'intéresse pas de regarder derrière."

Interview with Agnès Varda |

This interview took place on June 18, 2012, on the island of Noirmoutier off the coast of France.

AGNÈS VARDA: You know you should say the real title, *Lions Love* (. . . *and Lies*). Everyone always forgets the end bit . . . *and Lies*. I very much like the way titles resonate, even if it seems pointless (are we recording already?). Listen to this: that installation that was called *Ping Pong Tong et Camping*, it's very musical . . . it's the same with *Lions Love* (. . . *and Lies*)—I like it because it's a triplet and that was truly the subject. They wore their hair like lions, they wanted to invent love as three, and there were the lies in the news and on television, and also the true reality of the historical facts. I always like to position a story or fictional tale in the context where history has some meaning, history with a capital H. Even in *Cleo from 5 to 7* you see the fear of that boy who was walking with Cleo. He was a soldier in the war, even if we weren't fighting at that moment, he was in the Algerian war, a war he didn't want, one he never chose. That was the history of France in 1961.

KELLEY CONWAY: In my book, I focus on two major themes: your exemplary films and installations and also your shifting working methods through time. So, perhaps we could start with your working methods. What strikes me is that you seem to start your projects with considerable preparation but you also have a flair for improvisation. Do you see it that way also?

AV: Yes and no. Or no and yes, depending. Depending on the films. For example, when I started, when I felt the desire to make my first film, it was what I believe in America you would describe as "out of the blue," because for no reason I can give now, sixty years later, I went from photography to film.

I didn't go to the cinema. I'd seen very few films. Films written by Prévert I had seen and liked: *Quai des brumes* and *Les Enfants du paradis*. And I'd seen *The Idiot* because Gérard Philipe was in it and I knew Gérard from the Théatre National Populaire. So, I had no cinema culture, strictly none. No film school, no conferences. No internship or stint as a P.A. It's so unbelievable that when Alain Resnais was editing *La Pointe Courte* he asked me, "Have you been to the Cinémathèque [française] very often?" I didn't even know there was a *cinémathèque* in Paris on Avenue Messine. I'd never been.

It wasn't as if I was unaware of the artistic aspect, but I was completely without cinematic culture, utterly as if I'd just come out of the woods. So why did I want to make films? Let me think of a reason: I believe that I liked photography, but I also liked dialogue. Not necessarily talking, blabbing, but the idea of some kind of dialogue between people meant a lot to me. I saw one or two dreadful films such as *The Wages of Sin* because Jeanne Moreau was in them, playing a nurse who slept with someone, not sure who, it was one of those dark psychological dramas, as thick as this table. I thought it was awful.

On the other hand, I read a lot. We spoke of this the other day. After I had my *baccalauréat* from high school, I did not enroll in any university—rather, I said I would take a year to read. Because in school, there is no time for reading. We were four girls in an apartment that had been lent to us, a large studio full of books. Three of the girls set off to work every morning. Meanwhile, I, at nine every morning, because I still was on that scholastic timetable, at nine I would set myself at the table and read. I would stop for lunch, then I would take a little walk after (we lived near Pigalle). I read until the girls returned, then we would eat supper together. I read, rather systematically, again something we had not had time for in school. So obviously there were authors that aren't really that popular any more. Giraudoux, who wrote plays, Montherlant, André Gide, Mauriac, Malraux. Everything by Colette, without a second thought, everything . . . Obviously some poets as well . . . At times it was difficult. I found Mallarmé difficult. I was reading his biography.

For me, Baudelaire is still the prince of poets—I've never stopped reading Baudelaire.

English literature: I would read in translation, Virginia Woolf, and Joyce—so difficult. From America: Steinbeck, Hemingway. Dos Passos, the structure of his narratives made me want to make a film . . . And the one who made the strongest impression, Faulkner. In France, the *nouveau roman* had just appeared, there was Claude Simon, Robbe-Grillet, and at that time I still hadn't met Nathalie Sarraute, who I later met because she was the mother of Resnais's assistant editor.

I don't want to forget to tell you about the surrealist writers, André Breton, Max Jacob, Lautréamont, they absolutely meant a lot to me—and René Char, a hidden poet.

KC: You've said that Faulkner served as an inspiration for *La Pointe Courte*. Can you say more about that?

AV: I tell myself it's odd. I read some books where the authors created very difficult problems for themselves, in terms of the narrative structure, for example, Dos Passos, who jumps from one plotline to another, there's a form of rebound, like zapping . . . it seems to me he was trying to capture the world from all sides at once. And when I read *The Wild Palms*, I was totally impressed, because . . . you're familiar with the novel, it's this extraordinary saga of two convicts on a chain gang who escape when the Mississippi floods and who get lost; they get lost while escaping, and then there's this painful couple. This couple really struck me because—well first of all that story about the abortion . . . I need to reread it now, but I have difficulty reading now.

This couple has such an intense problem with their relationship. And that struck me rather heavily, in fact, because I saw that in life also, when you have a personal problem, it's love, [or] it's not love, something else, friendship, illness, and then, at the same time, there are social issues, politics, unions, activists, they don't all go together. People have all tried to be simultaneously in love and on strike, but it doesn't work. Either you're inside a small circle that is too intimate, or you're working with something collective and of general interest. Circles that never meet. Another thing that is really striking, not in the same way as *The Wild Palms*, is that the two stories never met, not in the same setting, nor in the subject matter—nothing. There were the convicts, there was the couple. Two worlds in separate and alternating chapters.

I remember very well that with thinking I was very clever, I said, very well, I'm going to read chapter 1, 3, 5, and 7. And then I'll read 2, 4, 6, and 8 to reach each storyline straight through. Yes, it's fascinating, but still, there's a reason for his artistic choice, and I reread it again in order, 1, 2, 3, 4, 5, 6 . . . So I in fact read it in three different ways. What I understood was that if there was no connection between these two stories, the juxtaposition of the two was critical, creating an effect of osmosis. I'm not sure how it permeates, at what level, how deeply within us. There are different flows, there are levels, and blends, and sometimes they hold together, and sometimes they flow, and sometimes they separate.

So this impression I felt so strongly, I said to myself, hey, if I can read a book like this, why not try to find an equivalent form of cinema?

KC: So Faulkner liked to create difficult problems?

AV: His writing was not overworked, but dense. It was difficult to read.

KC: Is that what you did with *La Pointe Courte*?

AV: Absolutely. The film is also difficult to read. I came across an interview I'd given at the time where I said that I'd decided to make a film that would read like a difficult book. I said that with a sharp awareness that it wouldn't work. It's odd, the word "work," when you say that a film "worked" or didn't "work." There are films that are prodigious, films that are playful, or films that are completely idle. Anyway . . .

There is, however, an expression I love: "To set the bar very high." You know . . . when high jumpers or pole vaulters put the bar higher and higher, higher even than they can jump. I don't mean to be pretentious, but I did set the bar very high when I started *La Pointe Courte*. A very artistic ambition.

KC: Yes. And that's something that is still evident in your work.

AV: Not in all my films. Not at all, because sometimes . . . for example, the opposite was true with *L'Une chante, l'autre pas*. Where I told myself that this was one film where I had to offer a message, and explanation. Without attempting to elevate the writing. So I chose to talk about ten years of struggle for contraception in France, the right to birth control, and secondly for a law authorizing that accident of contraception, which is abortion. It was ten years of struggle. I could tell that story through a fiction film because I had already made movies and unlike other women who experienced an awakening at that moment, my goal was not to be angry. My goal was not to say, my father did this to me, my brother did that, the doctor did this, and the law does that, even if it was true—there was much to reproach.

I tried to do it spoof-style, which is why the classic song of *L'une chante* is "It's not about papa anymore, nor the pope or king . . . not the judge or the doctor or the lawmaker." I can't recall all the words just now, something about making the lyrics and making the law. . . . But I know the refrain was "My body belongs to me," sung out. It was part of our message to sing these demands that were totally at the heart of this women's revolt, the idea that they should govern their own bodies.

You can only look back years later. Fifty years later and how are things now? In much of the world, women are still fully subject to their families, to religious law, to doctors, and to parents. And at home, we still have a lot of unresolved areas; some asked me, "What did I think of the jury selection at the Cannes film festival, where there were hardly any women."

I responded, "It seems to me that the fate of women in Egypt is more pressing than coming up with a list of films we like." That's what I really think. It's true though that the progress of women is slow. But I gave the media something to talk about, as I always do.

Let's return to Dos Passos, whose editing of phrases and chapters immediately make you think of film, and of Faulkner, with his strange approach to the conscious and unconscious. I was also very influenced by Giraudoux's dialogue; you may not be very familiar with it. He was a theater writer who was very important in the 50s. I wrote with a very light hand and great imagination, of course. Lots of references to mythology and legends . . . Amphitryon, Siegfried. It's been a while since I thought of Giraudoux. Later I discovered that I loved Ionesco's theater. The satire, the absurdity, and the innovative language.

KC: Did your work at the Théâtre National Populaire influence your films?

AV: Yes, I started out taking photos for Jean Vilar. It wasn't yet the Théâtre National Populaire. He started out by founding the Avignon Theater Festival. And then he brought Brecht to France. Nobody had performed Brecht in France.

KC: He was the first? I didn't know that.

AV: Yes. He brought *Mother Courage* in 1951. Brecht's wife, the actress Helene Weigel, came to make sure that we held the line, that we didn't betray Brecht, and so on. As it happened, artists like that began to change people's points of view, especially when you think of painting, when you see what the Cubists had done, that they had changed so much. With one portrait, you could see both the face and the profile.

I didn't love surrealist painting especially. But I loved Magritte, like all eight-year-old children. Because when he painted a pipe, he wrote "this is not a pipe."

Max Ernst is another I love. It was the spirit of surrealists, their attitude, their choices (Duchamps was amazing) and their texts that most affected me.

And then Picasso. Ah Picasso, he was certainly the painter that influenced me the most in my life, for the duration of my life. So much . . . Everything he did, but what impressed me particularly was that he reinvented himself. He was always looking for a new way, to be even more himself, but not to be more in fashion. He had moments where he returned to the classical. He made a series of very large drawings, totally classical, magnificent drawings, after which he tried something else. A real desire to work.

KC: You aren't so different. You reinvent yourself.

AV: I can't say that I did the same thing as Picasso, but I would have liked to . . .

KC: Still, you have always tried new things.

AV: Trying things that were still . . . How it speaks. How it reads. Whereas with Picasso, he wasn't afraid of scandal. Everyone mocked Picasso. People said, "Oh yes. Picassos." When we watch a child draw something . . . those beautiful drawings that only children can do, that we love, but they're a bit bizarre at times, that's when people say "Oh, it's a Picasso." But later, Picasso was called a genius . . .

Now there's great change, because museums have become democratized and are full of visitors, but when I first went to the Louvre, when I studied there in 1948, the museum was empty, or nearly so. There were small crowds on the weekends, just a little. Nowadays, it's all kinds of people, with no specific education, who visit museums and attend the major exhibits.

We were talking about the fact that painting had made some real leaps forward, Cubism, etc. As well as literature. Joyce, etc. But to the extent that I understood the cinema, even if I hadn't seen very many films, I always felt it was illustrating, a novel or a play, something like that. I immediately felt that the cinema had to be contemporary. I needed to invent *my* cinema. With *La Pointe Courte*, I just jumped in, in the most radical fashion. Two juxtaposed stories . . . one with the couple who are working out their relationship and then there were the lives of the fishermen, but I nevertheless had a bridge, I created a bridge between the two stories (so it wasn't entirely like Faulkner and *The Wild Palms*). The common point was the place itself, which is called *La Pointe Courte*.

I knew these fishermen. At that time, we didn't have little sound recorders, so when I finished at night, I took notes, recalling words they'd said, their stories. I spoke with many of them. There was a family, the Lubrano family, whom I adore, there were so many of them. Albert was the eldest, and his brother Louis, yes—the one I loved the most was Louis Lubrano, he was a distinguished man and we spoke often. I remember that I gave him *The Mirror of the Sea*, by Conrad, and he gave me time, he explained things to me. I knew his wife and children, obviously, but often we were in his shack, where he worked where he repaired the nets, because people are much more accurate, more real in the place where they work. So I had a lot of notes about the things he told me.

And I wanted to come up with a story. My narrative was based on the truth, but played by others, obviously. The brother played the father,

the husband—another played his father, or his grandfather. In any case
. . . the situation was such that they were suffering from competition
with the people of Etang de Thau, who were spreading rumors that the
water at La Pointe Courte was polluted, exactly where they fished for
shellfish. And there were even tests done by their so-called "enemies,"
in quotes. I thought that was critical, and in the scenario, I had them say,
"We need to get our own tests done." And that's what happened. For
the film, I told them: "Defend yourselves. Get a second test—it's not
certain at all that your water is polluted. And when the film was done,
that's what they did. Seriously, we got results, if I do say so, for the lives
of the fishermen, they had new tests done and everything was fine . . .
no one could prevent them from fishing.

KC: So you started with the fishermen's story and then added the
story of the couple?

AV: No both. Truly. From the start, there were two story lines for
the film. From the start. For the fishermen, I need to do some research,
and for the couple, I needed to write. How could I be acutely aware of
what it means to be a couple growing older? I had never really had a
relationship. I had lived more often communally.

KC: Back when you were reading a lot?

AV: Yes, when I was reading a lot, after graduating high school. The
others would head off to their work, their little jobs, and we'd see each
other at night.

On Sundays, we walked a lot, that's how I came to know Paris. We
would take the metro to Porte de Pantin station, then we'd walk. We
discovered the suburbs, we'd take the metro to Porte d'Aubervilliers and
walk, and I would think . . . I had this idea that it's not really the center,
it wasn't Notre Dame and St. Germain that would guide our lives, you
know.

Little by little I explored neighborhoods that now have become so
well known. You know the MK2 cinema at Quai de Loire? That neighborhood is beautiful, but fifty years ago, it was almost the outskirts of
the city; it was uninhabited. But there were tons and tons of factories
at that time, so there were many workers who were there, especially at
lunchtime, factory workers eating outside, sitting on a bench in the sun
and eating out of their lunchboxes.

Even near where I live now, rue Froidevaux. There was a big factory. There were all these guys in blue coveralls that were eating out of their lunchboxes against the wall of the Montparnasse cemetery, sitting in the sun. I have no pictures of that. Even though I was a photographer, I wasn't enough of one, you know, because I hadn't yet grasped that things would change. My neighborhood had extraordinary things, from another era. And then all at once, these things disappeared, and I would say, hmm, I never took any photos. I was a professional photographer but I never quite seized on the idea of taking pictures of my family, my neighbors in the 50s. I don't know why . . .

So I wrote my first film in my little courtyard on the rue Daguerre, Saturdays and Sundays when I'd finished my work as a photographer, I wrote the script that way. What effect does time have on a relationship? What makes this relationship crumble, weaken, distend or change itself, and how does it happen—what does it take?

Well, experience showed that in the trajectory of most relationships, there was a troubling dynamic, something slips, perhaps there is less desire, sometimes there is less continual attraction toward the other. So, studying other couples, this can evolve within that, clearly. But I tried to write it as a kind of crisis, and to place it within the landscape of La Pointe Courte. This was already a theme, this theme, which was also expressed in *Les Plages d'Agnès*: "If you open people, you'll find a landscape." So this particular man—he explains that if you opened him, you would find La Pointe Courte, and his father, a maritime carpenter, as well as boatbuilding. For me this guy, he was inhabited by . . . he resided in this interior landscape and he wanted his wife to get to know it, because she'd never come there.

The idea that knowledge of the other person must pass through the interior landscape housed in the other . . . perhaps there's nothing to what I'm saying. Yesterday, in fact, a reporter in Nantes asked me, "Why do you say landscape—what does it mean to have a landscape inside oneself?" I don't know, it's a favorite mental landscape, or significant landscape, or an obsessional landscape, I'm not sure which, exactly, but there was already an idea of that in *La Pointe Courte*, that she would know this man that she loved, but without knowing the landscape, right, and so she'd come for that. By coming there, she's understood something more about him.

KC: I can see that.

AV: It wasn't love at second sight, it was something that she didn't know, she didn't understand. I even pushed my idea that he should be associated with wood . . . And you know what, there was a man I adored there who was the father of three of my friends; he was a cabinetmaker and furniture seller in Sète. His name was Etienne, and I loved speaking with him because he loved his work. When I would go to his workshop, it smelled like wood. He even gave me an armchair that is still in my home on rue Daguerre. It was called a "Voltaire armchair," and he'd upholstered it in velvet.

He [the male character] wasn't a maritime carpenter in La Pointe Courte; there is a certain sliding of impressions, as always in a story, so I imagined this male character—"he"—who was the son of a carpenter at La Pointe Courte. I filmed all those little pieces of wood. We still see this everywhere in contemporary art. There's an American artist, Brigitte Stockholder, was it Brigitte? Maybe not, in any case, she exhibited pieces of plywood cut just so, and that was sixty years later.

So for me, those landscapes were his landscapes. She, on the other hand, for me, was pure Parisian, grating, which was why when she arrived and they were walking, we hear this train with the squealing breaks; for me she was associated with metal. What was truly extraordinary was the first time there was a public discussion of the film at the Studio Parnasse cinema, when it was released in 1956 (in that sole, tiny theater) there was a preview screening with a public discussion afterward. It was a Tuesday. In the theater were Truffaut, Marker, Nathalie Sarraute, Marguerite Duras! It was the cream of the intellectual set. And I was in the booth, looking out through the tiny window from high above in the projection booth. I never came down. I was—petrified, you know? Panicked. Hiding up there, but I was listening. And Chris Marker said, "Did anyone notice there was one element for him and one element for her?" He mentioned wood and metal. I was stunned. Stunned.

KC: Why, was it unconscious?

AV: No, it wasn't unconscious. Of course, I had really made him linked to wood, but this wasn't unconscious that I used this train with the noise of iron rails for her, who was . . . No, it wasn't unconscious, not at all. For me, he was at home, he was close to the wood, to the fishermen, while she arrived with her complaints, her dissatisfaction, she's grating . . . that's what I'd say. It was conscious, but I didn't think it was flagrant. I didn't think it showed. I thought it would be felt, perhaps. And Marker understood that.

And then after, already, there was something I did later, which was to use documentary images to say things one doesn't say, and that was *Documenteur*. You remember I talked to you about that. What I mean is what Emilie can't say, because she has a child, you don't explain solitude, romantic suffering, or waiting to a child, all of that. People waiting for a train, people in a Laundromat . . . these kinds of strangers who are all on the dock, who are fishing for who knows what. So there was already that, sometimes a bit heavy on the symbolism, there was already that in *La Pointe Courte*.

Because at a given moment we see an old bird, resting on a branch. And she says something very harsh; she says, "Our love is like an old romancer (*vieux beau*)." Do you know what that is, an old romancer? Those guys, you know, guys around sixty-five who are still very flirty, when people say "he was a great romancer of women," but they're a little old. You always see them at the beach resorts, that kind of place, you know? When she says, "Our love is like an old romancer," I showed a kind of . . . bird, an old bird resting on a branch, all stiff.

I often used the allegory where a mother loses her children, you know, a woman who has seven or eight children, and some of them die. So when this young child dies, we see a pair of hands that take a white net and throw it in tar, something we don't do anymore because all nets are made of nylon now. At one time, nets were made of white cotton and fishermen dyed them in tar, to strengthen them before putting them in the sea. Do you recall that little action?

So this white net becomes black when a child dies . . . It's not very light-handed. But it's already something I felt in '54, and that I repeated later, how documentary images nourish our silence. Documentary images, if we observe them, speak for us. That's showing in the place of telling. That's exactly the case in *Documenteur*, which I've shown you, where Emilie's emotions are expressed by documentary images I shot in Los Angeles.

In *La Pointe Courte* that's already there. At a given moment, they are talking about their love, which has faded; perhaps their desire also has faded. We see a lone fisherman on his boat, facing us, he dips a large pole into the water and he pushes and pushes toward the bottom to move the net on the bottom. If you watch that image, it's extremely sexual, when the guy is facing us like that, he repeats that gesture. I don't know if you noticed.

KC: Yes.

AV: You see, that image says something that isn't spoken, and that I want us to feel. Many of the images represent what this couple is experiencing when they're sitting, silent and discouraged. They are seeking their truth together, or the wound, I don't know which of the two suffers more from the idea of separating; their souls are tearing in silence. Behind them, a cat, then several cats, are scratching a wooden post and they turn and scratch. Obviously I was lucky, that's what I was hoping for because there were always cats in that neighborhood. So I said to the actors, "Sit there. Don't move, just wait." And we waited and the cat started scratching. And then another. It was gorgeous! When chance fulfills my expectation . . .

KC: Agnès, in one of your preparatory workbooks that you held on to from *Sans toit ni loi*, I read this sentence: "Less spectacle. More visual things." Or something like that.

AV: If you don't know what I wrote, I certainly don't know what I wrote. I don't remember.

KC: You were telling yourself, "Less narrative." It was a note to your . . .

AV: Oh, to myself.

KC: Yes, you wrote "less narrative" and "less psychology." So at a certain time, do you think that you explicitly tried to move away from that emphasis on character psychology?

AV: I was different on *Sans toit ni loi*; it was thirty years later! But I can tell you, with respect to the dialogue in *La Pointe Courte*, it was absolutely psychology, a psychological dialogue. That's how I started. And I also came from the world of theater . . .

KC: So that comes from theater? That kind of . . .

AV: I don't know. I took photos at the theater for three years. I was there every day. I had read Giraudoux, and classics like Corneille, Racine, and I discovered Brecht, I listened to the theater . . . And we even find, on occasion, one or two little reminiscences, for instance in

Cléo at a given moment. It's true, in *Cléo* there's a bit of slightly precious dialogue when she's talking with her lover. You know?

KC: Yes.

AV: When Angèle tells him "Oh! Don't put your hat on the bed!" He answers, "You are superstitious, ladies." "The gentleman would have noticed if he came more often." Angèle's character in *Cléo* is inspired by the classical theater, a little Diderot, a little bit. Later when both of them are sitting below the clocks, talking about him. It's exactly like the grande dame and her lady-in-waiting in all the great classics, you know. "So then, Angèle . . ." "so then, Madam . . ." You see, that's how it starts. So, sometimes things came out of my study of literature, rather adapted, but . . .

KC: So your time in the theater influenced your dialogue early on.

AV: Yes, and even when she says to her lover, "Cruel—and you said you loved me," which is a line from the theater. Racine I think. Just like when she's talking with the writer, Plumitif [lit. pencil-pusher or scribbler/hack]. She says, "He's horrid!" And she says, "Horrid is lovely, lovely is horrid." That's Shakespeare; what's the original in English? ["Fair is foul, and foul is fair"—Macbeth, act I, scene 1]—You know the quote, obviously.

KC: But in a much more modern context than classical literature . . . *Cléo* is a very modern film.

AV: Afterwards there was a big shift in my work, when I discovered the Californian counterculture, that was America in 1968, then again in '79–'80, with films like *Lions Love* (. . . *and Lies*) or *Documenteur*, features that were very different from my films shot in France. But I made a documentary in '80, *Mur murs*, in the same spirit as *Daguerréotypes* shot in Paris in 1975, in other words, a real documentary. Everyone loved *Daguerréotypes* a lot. I really listened to my neighbors, in the geographical bounds of immediate neighborhood. Because that always counts a lot for me, the geography of *Cléo*, her real trajectory through Paris, the geography of the little lanes of *La Pointe Courte* and the specific geography of *Daguerréotypes,* perhaps you read all that . . .

The fact that I inscribed that documentary within a ninety-meter limit to reach those who leave their doors open, that is to say the merchants. Because you can visit the neighbors two floors up, you can make a vertical slice of a house and talk to all the people on every floor; there are all kinds of methods.

In this case, I didn't intrude at home in their private lives. I met them where anyone could talk to them. You can go to the butcher's or the baker's, to the hairdresser's. The merchants within ninety meters of my home, my "block" in a way. So how to go about connecting the film? I've already said, I saw a Mystag poster [Mystag was a magician] in the window of a neighborhood café. In fact, you see the Mystag poster in the film. I realized that this was the great idea. Since there wasn't any cover charge, I said to the merchants, "All of you come! Come on, come on." And I filmed part of the show, and the merchants were there. So that gave me a link, I had a center, and so in the edit, I could return to the show and from there, head off to them. I didn't film all of the show, but I chose only those moments that were related to commerce. So when he changed water to wine, when he multiplied the number of bank notes, we thought about the exchange of money and coins in the shops; when he produced a fire, we thought of the baker, which is to say that I retained those elements in Mystag's show that served as a path, a link or bridge toward each merchant.

Obviously, when he hypnotizes them, he hypnotizes the weakest, obviously it was the hairdresser, who was the gentlest of men, and the weakest, and everyone knows that the trick is psychological; they manage to observe in the audience who should be called onstage to volunteer. He was clever. And he put the hairdresser to sleep, you know, with his neck and angles supported on two chairs, and clearly for me the general movement of the film was that all these lively characters were going to become still portraits, daguerreotypes. So Mystag put them to sleep.

From the beginning of the documentary, they were immobilized, set on their tradition of working as a couple. Right away we gather that they are not at all for progress, not at all for openness toward others, not at all in favor of everything I believe in, they just aren't. And that they are mesmerized in their thing, and that obviously in ending up with a portrait of these people, first of all, they are lovely portraits, but it's clear what it means—it means that they immobilize themselves, within society. Rather than politically and socially in their own lives, they become their own portrait.

Obviously I didn't know what I would film in each shop. With Nurith Aviv, that wonderful cinematographer, we were in the shops near the register; behind the register, the sound guy had set up his little mics and we waited for people to enter the shops. There was an intern who would signal us when someone was coming . . .

We would roll the camera, and nothing happened, nothing, nothing, and then someone would arrive and enter.

It was important that you have the impression we were always there, always. I heard you mention the word "method." One method is to try, or to give the impression that we were there even when no one came in, and the other method was to film those who entered, with, quote "less good things and good things." There were customers who came in, we filmed them, and they bought their meat and left—so, they weren't interesting; we saw that later while editing, so we cut it out.

I used the magician as a link for everything. When he pretended to cut himself, we then saw the butcher cutting meat, so that was slightly immediate, but it was effective.

There were so many hand movements in the magician's show that I subsequently filmed in equivalent amounts of commercial gestures and exchanges of money in close-ups. I also filmed the little wooden hand, you know, that was for gloves—so.

What I was able to observe was a social phenomenon: when I asked all these merchants where they came from, they came from Mayenne, Lower Brittany, Le Mans, Nantes, Sainte Pazanne. All these people came from the countryside and set up shop in Paris, in fact they settled very close to the Montparnasse Station, which served the region from whence they came.

KC: That's interesting.

AV: I conducted an experiment checking out the area near the Gare du Nord. They all came from the northern regions, at that time anyway, because now all those businesses are run by North Africans and Chinese, so we no longer have that cultural reference. But in my film, after asking them where they came from, I thought, I'll ask them what they dream of. And that too fascinated me, because even the word "dream" was beyond them. That is to say, there were those who said, well, "No we don't dream, we don't have time." Which is extraordinary. I mean, they have no idea that dreaming is a function, whether or not you can access it, but that it is a function of our sleep mechanism.

And so, this one, there were several . . . I don't think he spoke of dreams for example, the butcher, I believe, while the baker I believe spoke of insomnia, because he said, "You think of the dough not rising," you know, sometimes there are, we think about flour that rises, dough that doesn't, that sort of thing. The butcher's wife is the only one who said, "We dream of traveling, of idylls, and then we wake up and life is real again." And there were funny responses in the butcher's dreams, when he said "I dream of customers who ask me for a cut I don't have." That makes you smile . . .

I was lucky because within a block of my house you could get anything you needed: bread, meat, hardware, you know, household items, a hair salon, a grocer, a driving school, that wasn't a vital necessity but it was useful, as well as the notions/perfume bazaar.

KC: The perfume shop with the old couple . . .

AV: It was a bazaar like the old days. They sold notions, basic lingerie, little trinkets, lipsticks, and perfumes he mixed himself. Further up the road, there was a watch repairman, so clearly that came just at the right moment for my project. We find ourselves in the quandary of time in which I made the film and the time which stops for these merchants, who become immobilized when the magician puts them to sleep and I transform them to daguerreotypes.

KC: Yes, it's always about time.

AV: Yes, precisely.

KC: So, as far as your method was concerned, what about the installations? We're going to jump forward because . . .

AV: We're jumping from subject to subject, but there is continuity in what I'm telling you. Somewhat.

So why did I move from film to the installations? Because I always watched contemporary art, which is now often represented by installations, but it was already contemporary art when I saw it in the '60s in New York, "Underground Movies." I met Michael Snow, Brakhage, Sharitz, Jonas Mekas, all those marginal filmmakers.

KC: And Warhol, obviously, no?

AV: Ah, Warhol—I met him several times. First there was a meeting that Richard Roud had organized in New York. There were all the same people, Brakhage, Sharitz, there wa . . . Emshwiller, perhaps I'm pronouncing his name wrong, and Kenneth Anger, the scandal-monger . . .

KC: The great names of experimental filmmaking . . .

AV: And what I learned was that Michael Snow, who was there, at the time no one, or nearly no one was seeing those films, and he understood subsequently that he had to get his foot into the gallery world. Michael Snow began to sell to museums. Jonas Mekas also with films of his nonstop life. I was making movies in the normal distribution chain. Even my experimental films received normal distribution . . . marginal though that was.

Even *7 pièces . . . Cuisine*, which was so bizarre, it was released as the short before *Daguerreotypes* once, in a small cinema, but then, at least my films were seen. Those artists who began making installations, conquering the third dimension, not only the flat cinema screen.

KC: That's what interested you initially?

AV: For example, from the beginning I loved Boltanski, who installed light bulbs, the bulbs that hung above portraits. They were monuments, a bit like religious altarpieces. In his early career, he made an experimental film, *L'homme qui tousse.* Did you see that? There's a guy who's coughing, he has a coughing fit, he's coughing, coughing, he's sitting on the ground, coughing nonstop, it's fairly intolerable. He is an impressive artist. He did something new, we subscribed, we paid every two weeks to watch on a computer some original videos he made.

I had also been to Fresnoy; it's a video art and visual arts school in the north of France. The artist Alain Fleischer, who runs it, invited me to go up there. You meet the students a little bit and you can do good work, basically.

There was a great guy called Obrist. Hans Ulrich Obrist, who is very intelligent, created *Utopia Station* at the Venice Biennale in 2003, and he had clearly chosen people he liked a lot, such as Parreno, Pierre Huyghe, and then he wanted some small stars such as Yoko Ono, Lawrence Weiner, and many well-known artists. And he invited artists who weren't from the art world.

He invited a French-Martiniquais writer, he just died recently, Edouard Glissant, who wrote in a very complex manner; it was difficult to read but inventive. Very well known. Obrist said that because it was contemporary art, he invited me also and I wasn't part of the art world either . . .

Two years prior, he interviewed me. He made two huge books of interviews.

So I interested him, if I say so myself. Like everything that seemed important to him in world culture. Architects, artists, writers. And then these huge books in English, afterwards I found one that had been translated in French, with a very funny image on the cover, a caricature Obrist drew for . . . I don't know if . . . it wasn't Jeff Koons. I don't recall. In any case, he invited me to Venice, so there you have it. This happened, you see, after *Les Glaneurs et la glaneuse* with that image of a potato regerminating. . . . You know how this adventure started. I was observing what happens at the end of market day in the streets. I wondered "if people still gleaned" in the countryside, and I did a little investigating, wheat, corn, fruit, and I told myself, "I need to make a film about that," and I started to scout by telephone, calling farmers, calling people in the south because I wanted to go in every corner of the country, also to get different accents.

And so I realized that people still glean certain vegetables and fruit, and unfortunately, in the city, after street markets in the garbage cans. So I decided to film that systematically. And also I realized that artists recycle gleaning in works of art. For a long time now. If you take Picasso's goat, which you see in *Ulysses*, it is made with a basket, an old jerrycan, a bicycle handlebar, an iron box—you know? These artists always gleaned for objects and recycled in their own way.

When I began shooting, I started with potatoes, and the absolute luck I had on the second day, when I followed those trucks that were dumping "irregular" potatoes in the fields, and I came across a truck that was being emptied. There was this guy, you know, who was gathering the discarded potatoes because there are some clever people who gather them quickly and sell them cheaply in the housing projects, for instance.

This guy said to me: potato growers throw away everything that is too little, too big, anything monstrous. "Look," he said, "heart-shaped potatoes." And you recall, I filmed myself, saying "Oh, the heart, I want the heart." And that was incredibly lucky for me, because that second day of filming brought me what would become the meaning of the film, for me. That is to say, waste in the form of a heart.

There is an affection, and an empathy, that must emerge from that which is not only discarded, but "irregular" or odd-sized. And that interested me so much when the grower told me "We sell potatoes that are 5 cm by 7 cm in small three-kilo baskets. It's for supermarkets." "Everything that is odd-sized, we throw out." And all at once you get this little parable that in our society, everything that is odd-sized, irregular, you throw out. There you go.

Obviously, I started bringing heart-shaped potatoes home with me. I started putting them on glasses, on pieces of wood, on hollowed pumpkins to conserve them and watch them shrivel up. I have one right now. I developed a culture for the aging of potatoes, you could say. Because they are inedible. And another allegory: from all these old, abandoned things, emerges life, that kind of vital force that makes things sprout if you leave them in the air. If you put them in a box, it makes little cuttings that root.

I began to take photos of these potatoes, and I began to film them. And when Obrist proposed that I exhibit, I threw myself into this form that I love, the classical triptych, from antique painting, and I created one. In the middle, I placed a heart-shaped potato, which breathes a little when it moves, there's the noise of it breathing, and on the two side panels are filmed images, the adventures of sprouts, of rootings . . . all of this odd second life of potatoes.

So I decided to deposit real potatoes on the ground in front of the triptych, 700 kg worth. It was like the real mattresses I placed in the *Squatters* installation in Nantes, or like the sand on the *Bord de mer* [Seaside] that you saw. This idea that you can work on the representation that takes off from reality, and then one is brought back to reality. We evoke it, and then show it. It's like a method of thought. It begins with reality, and then you alter it, but don't forget it. So we spoke about *Utopia Station*, where I then presented *Patatutopia*. I was thrilled I was invited to participate in that. Obviously the Venice Biennale is a wonderful calling card. It was the best possible thing for me, you see.

KC: Will you answer another question for me?

AV: Go on. About my working method, which interests you, I answered in a certain fashion, but sometimes people make mistakes. I was often told, "You made a documentary because you saw Millet's famous painting, *The Gleaners . . .*" Not at all! I did it because people who go around gathering things off the ground intrigue me. The reference to this painting exists. I cited it and filmed it; it was only normal, everybody would have thought of it, but my subject was the true gleaners.

KC: Photography, cinema, now installations. Tell me more about the installations—is this a third lifetime for you?

AV: There won't be a fourth, unless I become a singer.

KC: Do it! I'd love to see that. What do installations represent for you, the opportunity to work with objects instead of only images?

AV: Actually, they explore space.

KC: Space. Is that what's critical to you?

AV: No, space is another use of the screen idea. I'm not the first to work with this. There are other examples, Fleischer, Snow. For example, I was interested in using a beach mattress as a screen for a color film that described the beach. Or rather, the real screen of *Veuves de Noirmoutier*, with 35mm film, shot by Éric Gauthier, the cinematographer who worked with Resnais, he shot *Les herbes folles*. In antique altarpieces, there are many small images around a large one. I did that. Around the large image of the widows on the beach, there are fourteen small monitors for the portraits.

In any case, this polyptych, that's how it's called, mixes yet again more classical filming, 35mm camera and all that, and what I discovered with *Les Glaneurs*, which was the possibility of filming myself at the moment when these small cameras appeared; that allowed me, in the case of the gleaners, to approach people in a precarious social position. I didn't want to show up with a team of three people and a sound boom . . .

I would say, "I need your testimony, I'm filming myself," and nearly all of them accepted more readily to speak. And then, some time after first speaking to me, I would say, for example, to the one who taught French to Malians, "Listen, can I come with a better camera and someone to record the sound because all alone, I can't film your class and record what you are saying." But since we'd already started working and it was going well, they would agree.

So I was lucky that these little cameras arrived just when I needed to take this approach. And sometimes, I would come into some kind of campground where there were gypsies, caravans, with my little camera, but with a tripod.

But since 2003, what have I added to my process? First, I can mix photography, cinema, and installation. I can combine all three. And then I've evolved: when I was young, people said, "Ah, wood, those lovely materials, pottery, leather." Those ancestral lovely materials. And all at once, I said: how beautiful plastic is! It brings color, and vitamin D, fantasy." This kind of burst of color that I adore. And so, I made this hymn, wouldn't you say, to plastic [in *Ping Pong Tong et Camping*]. I was even able to make columns—it's not the Parthenon but they're columns, with a base, and ooh, I piled up colored plastic containers, basins, machines, buckets, into a vertical jug.

For the color film that was projected on the mattress, I dressed people in a T-shirt or bathing suit without Mickey or Snow White and all that, nor pictures of singers or rock groups, nor slogans. Just colors, pure colors with that music by Bernard Lubat, which is wonderful. He was a very well-known jazz musician who attended the Uzeste Festival . . .

He worked at a table with two blowers below. He played piano without a piano, he played on the bare table and I amused myself by throwing ping-pong balls on the table in the middle of the music relayed by the blowers. I also made a slideshow with ordinary and sophisticated flip-flops bought for a euro, or sometimes up to four euros. They're pink, they're black with stripes . . . and then after, there were some that were more decorated, but overall, it's what you wear at the beach that costs the least. And I see so many things in fashion that annoy me—a very expensive slipper, a very expensive purse . . . Fashion photography. And I said, I'm going to do fashion photography with cheap flip-flops . . . You saw the series, they were beautiful!

There was one that had a sole like this, where I put stars and stripes, you saw that one. It had stripes in the sole, so I placed little stars cut out of paper, just for fun.

But clearly, it doesn't have the impact, in terms of emotion or meaning, that you get from the exhibitions you saw in Nantes on *Paroles des squatteurs* or even *Les Veuves*.

KC: Which both tell stories about people who are marginalized or forgotten.

AV: So, that means that there is, nevertheless, an important subject: widowhood or misery, and I was looking for a graphic or cinematographic means to express it.

KC: So, it's the structure . . .

AV: The structure that interests me, exactly, like the structure of the squatters, had been thought out before I filmed squatters over a period of three months. The widows also. I had made a little sketch that was an outline of the final presentation. I absolutely decided what I would film following this outline.

It was that huge old table that we set up on the beach of l'Épine. And I asked the widows to come. We went to pick them up in the car; we had bought cookies and fruit juice and all of that.

So based on the chosen structure, there is the work. Choose the models, choose the settings. But what is there before the structure? That we can't know. Why? Well, I know that with *Les Glaneurs*, I was in a café. I saw people who were gathering after the street market had packed up. I saw that every day, then one day I saw more clearly. We're thinking of nothing in particular, and then one day, a fixed notion. That's what struck me.

For *Daguerréotypes*, it was an old shop, le Chardon bleu, which was next to me on rue Daguerre, and one day, I stopped in front of the shop window and I looked so hard. I said to myself, dear God, there is the beginnings of something really strong here. They had decorated their window some twenty years before, and they hadn't touched it. I sometimes went into that shop with Rosalie [her daughter], we always bought some little thing. I had a certain amount of *carte blanche* with the German network, ZDF, so I asked them if I could tell a story about that shop and the couple who lived inside it, they said, "Why not?" And so I set off.

Sometimes there is something from the outside that is triggered. It's true that *La Pointe Courte* followed the structure of *Wild Palms*, that's certain. The structure was there before the story, before the scenario. And for *Sans toit ni loi*, also, it was truly the fact that you read in the papers that people were freezing to death, that had really struck me. They found an old woman at home who had frozen to death. We saw another poor man frozen under a doorway. I began to think, we're in the twentieth century, there are all kinds of heating: gas heating, even solar heating, electricity, wood fires, artificial fireplaces, and there are still people dying of the cold, as in the Middle Ages. So that was the first thought: the cold. Who dies from the cold?

Then after, the subject evolved toward people without a roof over their heads. It obsessed me so much. People without a home. There are these young vagrants, who wander. And I first though of a young vagrant on the road, he'll meet a girl, and then we'll leave him, and the film will continue on with her only, I thought about doing forty to forty-five minutes with this dropout boy, who wants nothing, etc. He meets a girl. He will perhaps spend a night with her, yes or no, whatever. There will be something, a conversation, or perhaps sex, or not, and when they separate, we'll leave with her. The film will only be her—and at the end, she dies frozen to death. That was the first version. Young women were really striking on the road, the ones I met.

KC: Setina.

AV: Setina, yes, but many others. To record her testimony, we filmed Setina in 16mm. Not very interesting. She didn't have very much to say; it was her behavior that was interesting, and the information she provided about how she survived all alone. Then I gave up on the idea of a boy and a girl. I decided it would be just a girl, Mona, and to really focus on the girl. And after, these were the essential themes for me: the cold, and dirtiness. How the filth starts; she comes out of the water, she's clean, but she gets filthier and filthier, more and more until that ultimate filth that is the Festival of Cournonterral. The game in this festival is to dirty characters all dressed in white. Mona is pursued with muddy rags, and she loses all sense of direction. She has already lost her blanket, which was her shelter.

At the same time, as the filth gains ground, the cold also gains ground, and she loses everything. She loses speech, and begins to move toward an awful solitude.

KC: It's not a conventional portrait.

AV: Was I able to paint her portrait? Because my idea was that we can't grasp a person. We can never fully understand another person. I was trying to get the portrait of the young, ungraspable Mona. It was a portrait in fragments, through the testimony of people who saw her pass by. And they'll say, "Oh, for me she was a whore. Oh, a free girl—Oh what a great girl—Oh poor thing—Oh she was so funny . . ." So the un-graspable portrait will be determined by people who will speak of her. And since we never know everything, and even I, as the scenarist, I don't want to be a demiurge. I don't know everything about the characters I invent.

I don't want to know where she comes from, why she's alone on the road . . . there are two possibilities for imagining where she came from and I don't want to tell them. What interests me is that during the film, we learn more about those who saw her pass by, and who passed some judgment about her. I describe to some extent the state of mind of rural society in this part of the south of France. One day, in a public debate, a French professor said, "This is entirely like the ending of a Stendhal novel . . ." Which one—*Le Rouge et le noir*? He says, "A novel's character is a mirror who walks along the road." That's extraordinary. Because we learn much more about this xenophobic society than about her. That was a wonderful line. He was a French professor who quoted it to me, and I said thank you. I read the novel, but I don't remember that line. The theme of the mirror interests me because Mona is the mirror of a society that rejects her. And she is nothing. She is a denial and she is a nothing more than the walking mirror. And she dies, and we conclude our interview about this solitary death.

La Pointe Courte (1955)
Fiction
France
Production: Ciné-Tamaris
Producer: Agnès Varda
Screenplay: Agnès Varda
Technical Advisor: Carlos Vilardebo
Artistic Advisor: Valentine Schlegel
Cinematography: Louis Stein
Editor: Alain Resnais, Anne Sarraute
Sound: Georges Mardiguian
Music: Pierre Barbaud
Cast: Philippe Noiret (man); Silvia Monfort (woman); the inhabitants of La Pointe Courte
35mm
Black and white
80 minutes

Ô saisons, Ô chateaux (1958)
Documentary
France
Production: Films de la Pléiade
Commissioned by the Office National du Tourisme
Producer: Pierre Braunberger
Cinematography: Quinto Albicocco
Editor: Janine Verneau
Music: André Hodeir
Commentary spoken by Danièle Delorme
Poems spoken by Antoine Bourseiller
Poems by Pierre de Ronsarad, Charles d'Orléans, François Villon, and Clément Marot

Film extract: *L'Assassinat du Duc de Guise* (Charles Le Bargy and André
  Calmettes, 1908)
Gowns: Jacques Heim
35mm
Eastmancolor
22 minutes

L'Opéra-Mouffe (1958)
Documentary
France
Production: Ciné-Tamaris
Producer: Agnès Varda
Cinematography: Agnès Varda and Sacha Vierny
Editor: Janine Verneau
Music: George Delerue
With the participation of Dorothée Blank, José Varela, Jean Tasso, Antoine
  Bourseiller, and the inhabitants and shopkeepers of the rue Mouffetard in
  the 5th arrondissement of Paris
Stanzas written by Agnès Varda
16mm
Black and white
17 minutes

Du côté de la côte (1958)
Documentary
France
Production: Argos Films
Producers: Anatole Dauman and Philippe Lifschitz
Commissioned by the Office National du Tourisme
Cinematography: Quinto Albicocco
Editor: Henri Colpi
Music: Georges Delerue
Commentary by Agnès Varda, spoken by René Coggio and Anne Olivier
Song by Agnès Varda and Georges Delerue performed by Jean-Christophe
  Benoit
35mm
Eastmancolor
24 minutes

Cléo de 5 à 7 (*Cleo from 5 to 7*; 1962)
Fiction
France
Production: Rome Paris Films

Producer: Georges de Beauregard and Carlo Ponti
Screenplay: Agnès Varda
Cinematography: Jean Rabier
Sound: Julien Coutelier
Art Direction: Bernard Evein
Editor: Janine Verneau
Sound:
Music and Songs: Michel Legrand and Agnès Varda
Cast: Corinne Marchand (Cléo); Antoine Bourseiller (Antoine, the soldier);
Dominique Davray (Angèle); Dorothée Blank (Dorothée); Michel Legrand
(Bob); Serge Korber (Plumitif); José-Luis de Vilallonga (Cléo's lover)
35mm
Black and White/Color
90 minutes

Salut les Cubains (*Hi There, Cubanos*, 1964)
Documentary
France
Production: Société Nouvelle Pathé-Cinéma
Animation and camerawork: J. Marques and C. S. Olaf
Still images: Agnès Varda
Editor: Janine Verneau
Commentary spoken by Michel Piccoli and Agnès Varda
35mm
Black and White
30 minutes

Le Bonheur (*Happiness*, 1965)
Fiction
France
Production: Parc Films
Producer: Mag Bodard
Screenplay: Agnès Varda
Cinematography: Jean Rabier and Claude Beausoleil
Sound: Louis Hochet
Set Decoration: Hubert Monloup
Editor: Janine Verneau
Cast: Jean-Claude Drouot (François); Claire Drouot (Thérèse); Marie-France
Boyer (Emilie)
Eastmancolor
82 minutes

Elsa la Rose (1966)
Documentary
France
Production: Pathé Cinéma and Ciné-Tamaris
Cinematography: Willy Kurant, William Lubtchansky
Sound: Bernard Ortion
Music: Simonovitch, Ferrat, Moussorgsky, Gershwin, Handy
Poems by Louis Aragon voiced by Michel Piccoli
Cast: Louis Aragon (himself); Elsa Triolet (herself)
16mm
Black and White
20 minutes

Les Créatures (*The Creatures*, 1966)
Fiction
France
Production: Parc Films; with the support of Madeleine Films, Sandrew, Franscope
Producer: Mag Bodard
Screenplay: Agnès Varda
Cinematography: Willy Kurant and William Lubtchansky
Décor: Claude Pignot
Editor: Janine Verneau
Music: Pierre Barbaud and Purcell
Cast: Catherine Deneuve (Mylène); Michel Piccoli (Edgar); Lucien Bodard (Ducasse)
35mm
Black and White / Color
105 minutes

Loin du Vietnam (*Far from Vietnam*, 1967)
Documentary
France
Production: S.L.O.N.
Collective film by Jean-Luc Godard, Joris Ivens, William Klein, Claude Lelouch, Alain Resnais, and Agnès Varda. Varda's contribution was not retained in the film's final version.
Black and White / Color
120 minutes

Uncle Yanco (1968)
Documentary
France

Assistant Director: Tom Luddy
Cinematography: David Myers
Sound: Paul Oppenheim
Editor: Jean Hamon
Music: Richard Lawrence, Yannis Spanos, and Albinoni
35mm
Color
22 minutes

Black Panthers (1970)
Documentary
France
Shot in 1968, rejected by ORTF (Office de Radiodiffusion Télévision Française), and shown with *Lions Love (and Lies)* at Studio Parnasse in Paris in 1970.
Production: Ciné-Tamaris
Producer: Agnès Varda
Assistant: Tom Luddy
Cinematography: David Myers, Paul Aratow, John Shofill, Agnès Varda
Sound: Paul Oppenheim, James Steward
Editor: Paddy Monk
With Stokely Carmichael, Eldridge Cleaver, Huey Newton, and Bobby Seale
16mm
Black and White
28 minutes

Lions Love (and Lies) (1969)
Fiction
USA/France
Production: Ciné-Tamaris and Max L. Raab Productions
Producer: Agnès Varda
Screenplay: Agnès Varda
Cinematography: Steve Larner
Editor: Robert Dalva
Sound: Georges Alch
Music: Joseph Byrd
Cast: Gerome Ragni (Jim); James Rado (Jerry); Viva (Viva); Shirley Clarke (Shirley Clarke)
Color
35mm
110 minutes

Daguerréotypes (1975)
Documentary

West Germany/France
Production: Ciné-Tamaris, Institut National de l'Audiovisuel (INA), Zweites
    Deutsches Fernsehen (ZDF)
Cinematography: Nurith Aviv and William Lubtchansky
Sound: Antoine Bonfanti
Editor: Gordon Swire
16mm
Eastmancolor
80 minutes

Réponse de femmes (*Women Reply*, 1975)
Documentary
France
Production: Antenne 2 (for the television program *F comme femme*)
Screenplay: Agnès Varda
Cinematography: Jacques Reiss, Michel Thiriet
Sound: Bernard Bleicher
Montage: Marie Castro
16mm
Color
8 minutes

Plaisir d'amour en Iran (1977)
France
Production: Ciné-Tamaris
Screenplay: Agnès Varda
Cinematography: Nurith Aviv and Charles Van Damme
Editor: Sabine Mamou
Sound: Henri Morelle
Cast: Valérie Mairesse (Pomme); Ali Rafie (Ali Darius)
Commentary spoken by Thérèse Liotard
35mm
Color
6 minutes

L'une chante, l'autre pas (*One Sings, the Other Doesn't*, 1977)
Production: Ciné-Tamaris with the support of Société Française de Production,
    INA, Contrechamp, Paradise Film, Population Film
Distribution: Gaumont / Ciné-Tamaris
Cinematography: Charles Vandamme, Nurith Aviv
Sound: Henri Morelle
Set Decoration and Costume: Frankie Diago
Music and Songs: François Wertheimer et Orchidée

Lyrics: Agnès Varda
Editor: Joëlle Van Effenterre
Cast: Valérie Mairesse (Pomme); Thérèse Liotard (Suzanne); Robert Dadiès
   (Jérôme); Jean-Pierre Pellegrin (Pierre Aubanel); Ali Raffi (Darius); François
   Wertheimer (François, the flutist); the Orchidée Group: Micou Papineau,
   Doudou Greffier, Joëlle Papineau
35mm
Eastmancolor
120 minutes

Mur Murs (1982)
Documentary
France
Production: Ciné-Tamaris with the participation of Fonds de Création Audio-
   visuelle du Ministère de la Culture et de la Communication; Antenne 2;
   Janus (Frankfurt)
Cinematography: Bernard Auroux
Sound: Lee Alexander
Editor: Sabine Mamou
Documentation: Alain Ronay and Denise Warren
Music: Buxtehude, Carey, Cruz, Fiddy, Healy, Lauber, Los Illegals, Parker
16 and 35mm
Color
81 minutes

Documenteur (1982)
Fiction
France
Production: Ciné-Tamaris
Cinematography: Nurith Avi
Sound: Jim Thornton, Lee Alexander
Music: Georges Delerue
Editor: Sabine Mamou
Cast: Sabine Mamou (Émilie Cooper); Mathieu Demy (Martin Cooper); Lisa
   Blok (Lisa); Tom Taplin (Tom Cooper)
16mm
Color
63 minutes

Ulysse (1982)
Documentary
France
Production: Garance / Agnès Varda with the participation of Paris Audiovisuel,
   Antenne 2 and the CNC

Photographs: Agnès Varda
Camera: Jean-Yves Escoffier
Sound: Jean-Paul Mugel
Music: Pierre Barbaud (extract from *La Pointe Courte*)
Editor: Marie-Jo Audiard
With Ulysse Llorca, Bienvenida Llorca, Fouli Elia
35mm
Black and White
22 minutes

Une Minute pour une image (One Minute for One Image, 1983)
Documentary (Television Series)
France
Production: Garance, Centre National de la Photographie (Robert Delpire),
 FR3, with the participation of the Ministère de la Culture
Choice of photographs and commentators: Agnès Varda
Commentaries by Agnès Varda, Marguerite Duras, Yves Montand, Delphine
 Seyrig, Yves Saint Laurent, and Hervé Guilbert
Editing: Marie-Jo Audiard, Sabine Franel, Cévanne Haicault
35mm
Black and White
170 programs lasting one to two minutes each; broadcast from January 31 to
 July 22, 1982

Les Dites Cariatides (The So-Called Caryatids, 1984)
Documentary
France
Production: Ciné-Tamaris, TF1
Commissioned by TF1 for the program *Domino*
Executive Producer: Teri Wehn-Damish and Bertrand Gauthier
Commentary: Agnès Varda
Poems by Charles Baudelaire
Music: Rameau played by Jean-Charles Guriand; Offenbach sung by François
 Wertheimer
16mm/35mm
Eastmancolor
13 minutes

7 P., cuis., s. de b . . . (à saisir) (1984)
Fiction
France
Production: Ciné-Tamaris with the support of C.N.A.P., Ministère de la Culture
 (F.I.A.C.R.E.)

Filmed at the former Hospice de Saint-Louis d'Avignon during the exhibition "Le Vivant et l'artificiel" by Louis Bec
Screenplay: Agnès Varda
Cinematography: Nurith Aviv
Sound: Daniel Ollivier
Music: Pierre Barbeau (from *Les Créatures*, 1965)
Editor: Sabine Mamou
Cast: Yolande Moreau (Belgian servant); Marthe Jarnias (old woman); Hervé Mangani (father #1); Louis Bec (father #2); Saskia Cohen-Tanugi (young mother); Colette Bonnet (older mother); Catherine de Barbeyrac (older daughter); Pierre Esposito (older son); Folco Chevalier (boyfriend); Michèle Nespoulet (good servant)
35mm
Color
27 minutes

Sans toit ni loi (*Vagabond*, 1985)
Fiction
France
Production: Ciné-Tamaris with the participation of the Ministère de la Culture, Film 4, C.M.C.C.
Screenplay: Agnès Varda
Cinematography: Patrick Blossier
Sound: Jean-Paul Mugel
Set Decoration: Jean Bauer, Anne Violet
Music: Joanna Bruzdowicz
Editing: Agnès Varda and Patricia Mazuy
Cast: Sandrine Bonnaire (Mona); Macha Méril (Madame Landier); Stéphane Freiss (Jean-Pierre); Yolande Moreau (Yolande); Patrick Lepczynski (David); Yahiaoui Assouna (Assoun); Joël Fosse (Paulo); Marthe Jarnias (Aunt Lydie); Laurence Cortadellas (Éliane); and the inhabitants of the Nîmes region
35mm
Color
105 minutes

T'as de beaux escaliers . . . tu sais (*You've Got Beautiful Stairs, You Know*, 1986)
Documentary
France
Production: Ciné-Tamaris and Miroirs for the Cinémathèque française; with the participation of Isabelle Adjani
Cinematography: Patrick Blossier
Music: Michel Legrand
Editor: Marie-Jo Audiard

35mm
Color
3 minutes

Jane B. par Agnès V. (1988)
Fiction
France
Production: Ciné-Tamaris and La Sept
Screenplay: Agnès Varda
Cinematography: Nurith Aviv, Pierre-Laurent Chenieux
Sound: Olivier Schwob, Jean-Paul Mugel, Alix Comte
Set Decoration: Bertrand Lheminier
Costumes: Rosalie Varda, Rose-Marie Melka
Editing: Agnès Varda, Marie-Jo Audiard
Cast: Jane Birkin (Calamity Jane, Joan of Arc, et al.); Philippe Léotard (painter/
murderer); Jean-Pierre Léaud (angry lover); Serge Gainsbourg (himself);
Charlotte Gainsbourg (herself); Alain Souchon (reader of Verlaine); Laura
Betti (Lardy); Farid Chopel (colonialist); Mathieu Demy (himself)
35mm
Black and White/Color
97 minutes

Kung-Fu Master (1988)
Fiction
France
Production: Ciné-Tamaris and La Sept
Cinematography: Pierre-Laurent Chenieux
Sound: Olivier Schwob
Music: Joanna Bruzdowicz
Editor: Marie-Jo Audiard
Cast: Jane Birkin (Mary-Jane); Mathieu Demy (Julien); Charlotte Gainsbourg
(Lucy); Lou Doillon (Lou); Judy Campbell (mother); David Birkin (father);
Andrew Birkin (brother)
35mm
Color
80 minutes

Jacquot de Nantes (1991)
Fiction-Documentary
France
Production: Ciné-Tamaris
Screenplay: Jacques Demy and Agnès Varda
Cinematography: Patrick Blossier, Agnès Godard, Georges Strouvé

Sound: Jean-Pierre Duret, Nicolas Naegelen
Music: Joanna Bruzdowicz
Set Decoration: Robert Nardone, Olivier Radot
Costumes: Françoise Disle
Editor: Marie-Jo Audiard
Documentation : Mireille Henrio
Cast: Philippe Maron (Jacquot 1); Édouard Joubeaud (Jacquot 2); Laurent
   Monnier (Jacquot 3); Brigitte De Villepoix (mother); Daniel Dublet (father)
35mm
Color/Black and White
118 minutes

Les Demoiselles ont eu 25 ans (*The Young Girls Were 25 Years Old*, 1993)
Documentary
France
Production: Ciné-Tamaris with the support of the CNC and the Commission
   Télévision de la Procirep
Cinematography: Stéphane Krausz and George Strouvé
Color images (1966): Agnès Varda
Video Images: Alexandre Auffort
Music: Michel Legrand, Jacques Loussier
Editing: Agnès Varda, Anne-Marie Cotret
With Mag Bodard, Catherine Deneuve, Jacques Perrin, Bertrand Tavernier,
   Bernard Evein, Jean-Louis Frot, Michel Legrand
16mm and 35mm
Color
63 minutes

L'Univers de Jacques Demy (*The World of Jacques Demy*, 1993/1995)
Documentary
France
Production: Ciné-Tamaris with the support of the CNC, Ministère des Affaires
   Étrangères, INA, Canal+, Canal+ France/Belgium/Spain, Docstar; in associa-
   tion with Sofica Valor 2.
Cinematography: Stéphane Krausz et Georges Strouvé
Editor: Marie-Jo Audiard
Music: Michel Legrand, Michel Colombier
Sound: Thierry Ferreux, Jean-Luc Rault-Cheynet, Nathalie Vidal
With Catherine Deneuve, Michel Piccoli, Jeanne Moreau, Anouk Aimée, Dani-
   elle Darrieux, Jacques Perrin, Richard Berry, Françoise Fabian, Dominique
   Sanda, Jean-François Stévenin
35mm
Color
90 minutes

Les Cent et une nuits (*One Hundred and One Nights*, 1995)
Fiction
UK/France
Production: Ciné-Tamaris, France 3 Cinéma (Paris), Recorded Picture Cy Ltd
 (London), with the support of Canal+, the CNC, Procirep and A.R.P.
Cinematography: Éric Gautier
Sound: Henri Morelle, Jean-Pierre Duret
Set Decoration: Cyr Boitard, Cédric Simoneau
Costumes: Rosalie Varda
Music: Maurice Jarre, Michel Legrand, Nino Rota, Michel Colombier
Editor: Hugues Darmois
Cast: Michel Piccoli (Simon Cinéma); Marcello Mastroianni (the Italian friend);
 Henri Garcin (Firmin); Julie Gayet (Camille); Mathieu Demy (Mica)
35mm
Color
135 minutes

Les Glaneurs et la glaneuse (*The Gleaners and I*, 2000)
Documentary
France
Production: Ciné-Tamaris with the support of the CNC, Canal+, and Procirep
Cinematography: Stéphane Krausz, Didier Rouget, Didier Doussin, Pascal
 Sautelet, and Agnès Varda
Sound: Emmanuel Soland
Music: Joanna Bruzdowicz, Pierre Barbaud, Isabelle Olivier (Ocean), François
 Wertheimer, Rap: Bredel and Klugman
Editor: Agnès Varda, Laurent Pineau
Digital Video/35mm
Color
82 minutes

Deux ans après (*Two Years Later*, 2002)
Documentary
France
Production: Ciné-Tamaris with the participation of Canal+
Cinematography: Stéphane Krausz and Agnès Varda
Music: Joanna Bruzdowicz, Isabelle Olivier (Océan), Georges Delerue, Richard
 Klugman, François Wertheimer
Editor: Agnès Varda
Video
Color
64 minutes

Le Lion volatil (*The Volatile Lion*, 2004)
Fiction
France
Production: Ciné-Tamaris
Cinematography: Mathieu Vadepied, Xavier Tauveron
Sound: Jean-Luc Audy
Editing: Agnès Varda, Sophie Mandonnet
Cast: Julie Depardieu (apprentice clairvoyant); David Deciron (employee at the catacombs); Frédérick E. Grasser-Hermé (clairvoyant); Valérie Donzelli (the customer in tears)
35mm
Color
12 minutes

Ydessa, les ours et etc. (*Ydessa, the bears, and etc.*, 2004)
Documentary
France
Production: Ciné-Tamaris with the support of France 5, France 2, the Jeu de paume, the Ministère de la communication and the Centre National des Arts Plastiques
Cinematography: Markus Seitz, John Holosko, Claire Duguet, Rick Kearney
Sound: Jens-Christian Börner, Rob Fletcher, Jason Milligan
Music: Didier Lockwood et Isabelle Olivier (Océan)
Editing: Agnès Varda, assisted by Jean-Baptiste Morin
35mm (in Munich) / Video (in Toronto)
Color
44 minutes

Les Plages d'Agnès (*The Beaches of Agnès*, 2008)
Documentary
France
Production: Ciné-Tamaris and ARTE France Cinéma; with Canal+, Région Ile-de-France, Région Languedoc-Roussillon, CNC
Producer: Agnès Varda
Distribution: Les Films du Losange
Cinematography: Alain Sakot, Hélène Louvart, Arlène Nelson, Julia Fabry, Jean-Baptiste Morin, and Agnès Varda
Sound: Pierre Mertens, Olivier Schwob, Frédéric Maury
Music: Joanna Bruzdowicz, Stéphane Vilar, Paule Cornet
Production Design: Franckie Diago
Editing: Agnès Varda with Baptiste Filloux and Jean-Baptiste Morin
Digital Video/35mm
Color
110 minutes

Agnès de ci de là Varda (*Agnès Varda Here and There*, 2011)
Documentary (TV Series)
France
Production: Ciné-Tamaris and ARTE with the support of the CNC
Screenplay: Agnès Varda
Cinematography: Agnès Varda and Julia Fabry
Editing: Johan Boulanger, Jean-Baptiste Morin, Agnès Varda
Sound: Jean-Lionel Etcheverry
Music: Laurent Levesque
With Chris Marker, Pierrick Sorin, Anouk Aimée, Manoel de Oliveira, Michel
    Piccoli, Aleksandr Sokurov, Hans Obrist, Miquel Barcelò, Christian Boltanski,
    Annette Messager, Pierre Soulages, and Jean-Louis Trintignant
Video
Color
Five Episodes, forty-five minutes each; broadcast December 19–23, 2011.

Bibliography |

The best source of information on Agnès Varda's work and working methods is the private archive of Ciné-Tamaris, Varda's production company, which contains planning notes, scripts, still images, posters, reviews, letters, and other material for each of her films and installations. The archive at Ciné-Tamaris is organized by film title. As a result, when I refer to an unpublished document I consulted at the archive, I cite Varda's name, Ciné-Tamaris Archive, and the title of the work in question.

Varda's autobiography, *Varda par Agnès* (Paris: Cahiers du cinéma, 1994) offers an unusually rich account of a filmmaker's inspirations and mode of production as well as credits, extracts of reviews, and a filmography through 1994. Also essential are Varda's supplements for her DVD collections: *Varda Tous Courts* (Ciné-Tamaris); *4 by Agnès Varda*, the boxed set of DVDs containing *La Pointe Courte, Cleo from 5 to 7, Le Bonheur*, and *Vagabond* (Criterion Collection); and *Tout(e) Varda*, her complete works on DVD (Arte Editions).

Abel, Richard. *The French Cinema: The First Wave, 1915–1929*. Princeton, N.J.: Princeton University Press, 1984.
Alion, Yves. "Entretien avec Agnès Varda." *L'Avant-scène Cinéma* 526 (November 2003): 3–9.
Baecque, Antoine de. *Les Cahiers du cinéma: Histoire d'une revue.* Vol. 1. Paris: Editions Cahiers du cinéma, 1991.
———. *La Cinéphilie, Invention d'un regard, histoire d'une culture, 1944–1968*. Paris: Fayard, 2003.
Balsom, Erika. *Exhibiting Cinema in Contemporary Art*. Amsterdam: Amsterdam University Press, 2013.
Bastide, Bernard. "Agnès Varda: entre la côte et la cocotte (d'Azur), 1ère partie." *Ciné Nice* 21, 3eme trimestre (2009).

————. "Genèse et reception de Cléo de 5 à 7 d'Agnès Varda." Dissertation, Université de Paris III, 2006.

————. "*La Pointe Courte* ou comment réaliser un film à Sète (Héraut) en 1954." *Cahiers de la Cinémathèque* 61 (1994): 31–36.

Bazin, André. "La Pointe Courte." *La Cinématographie française* 15 (May 9, 1955).

————. "La Pointe Courte: Un film libre et pur." *Parisien Libéré*, January 7, 1956.

————. "Petit Journal Intime du cinéma." *Cahiers du cinéma* (August–September 1955).

Beaches of Agnès. Promotional material. Roissy Films, 2008.

Bénézet, Delphine. *The Cinema of Agnès Varda: Resistance and Eclecticism.* London and New York: Wallflower Press and Columbia University Press, 2014.

Benoliel, Bernard. "La main de l'autre." *Cahiers du cinéma* 548 (July–August 2000): 63.

Benoist, Olivier. "Stéphane Krausz, Glaneur d'Images pour Agnès Varda." *Le Technicien Film & Video* 505 (Nov. 15–Dec. 15, 2000): 24–27.

Beylie, Claude. "Le Triomphe de la Femme." *Cahiers du cinéma* (April 11–17, 1962): 26.

Billard, Pierre. "*Cléo de 5 à 7.*" *Cinéma 62* 67 (June 1962): 117–18.

Bluher, Dominique. "Autobiography, (Re)enactment and the Performative Self-portrait in Varda's *Les Plages d'Agnès / The Beaches of Agnès* (2008)." *Studies in European Cinema* 10.1 (2013): 59–69.

Bordwell, David. "The Art Cinema as a Mode of Film Practice." In *Poetics of Cinema*, 151–69. New York: Routledge, 2008.

Bory, Jean-Louis. "Ce qu'il a de changé au cinéma depuis dix ans." *Arts* 874 (June 20–26, 1962).

————. "*Cléo de 5 à 7* est un chef d'oeuvre." *Arts* (April 1962).

————. "Pourquoi nous avons choisi Cléo de 5 à 7." *Arts* 862 (March 28–April 3, 1962).

Bouffard, Véronique. "Les Glaneurs et la glaneuse: Agnès Varda ou le bonheur de filmer." *La Lettre d'Unifrance*, January 25, 2001, 19–22.

Burnett, Colin. *The Invention of Robert Bresson: Cinephilia, the Avant-Garde and the Making of the Auteur.* Bloomington: Indiana University Press, Forthcoming.

Calatayus, Agnès. "The Self-Portrait in French Cinema," In *Textual and Visual Selves*, edited by Natalie Edwards, Amy L. Hubbell, and Ann Miller, 209–33. Lincoln: University of Nebraska Press, 2011.

Callenbach, Ernst. "The Gleaners and I (Les Glaneurs et la glaneuse)." *Film Quarterly* 56.2 (Dec. 20, 2002): 46–49.

Charensol, Georges. "Le Coeur Révélateur." *Lettres françaises* 922 (April 12–18, 1962).

————. "La Pointe-Courte." *Nouvelles Littéraires*, January 19, 1956.

Chevalier, Jacques. "Passé et present des cinés-clubs." In *Regards neufs sur le cinéma*, edited by Jacques Chevalier and Max Egly, 242–52. Paris: Peuple et culture, Seuil, 1963.

"Cléo a conquis la province," *Arts* 869 (May 16–22, 1962).

"Le Club des avant-premières." *Arts* 868 (May 9–15, 1962).

"Comment adhérer au club?" *Arts* 862 (March 28–April 3, 1962).

Conway, Kelley. "The New Wave in the Museum: Varda, Godard, and the Multi-Media Installation." *Contemporary French Civilization* 32:2 (Summer 2008): 195–217.

———. "Responding to Globalization: The Evolution of Agnès Varda." *SubStance* 43.1 (2014): 109–22.

———. "Varda at Work." *Studies in French Cinema* 10.2 (2010): 125–39.

Crisp, Colin. *The Classic French Cinema, 1930–1960*. Bloomington: University of Indiana Press, 1997.

Darke, Chris. "Refuseniks." *Sight & Sound* 11:1 (January 2001): 30–33.

Davay, Paul. "La Pointe Courte." *Les Beaux Arts* 27 (April 1956).

Denoyan, Gilbert. Radio interview with Agnès Varda. "Zappinage." France Inter, March 26, 1992.

DeRoo, Rebecca. "Confronting Contradictions: Genre Subversion and Feminist Politics in Agnès Varda's *One Sings, the Other Doesn't*." *Modern and Contemporary France* 17:3 (August 2009): 249–65.

———. "Unhappily Ever After: Visual Irony and Feminist Strategy in Agnès Varda's *Le Bonheur*." *Studies in French Cinema* 8.3 (Fall 2008): 189–209.

"Deuxième Spectacle du Club des Avant-Premières: *Le Fleuve Sauvage* d'Elia Kazan." *Arts* 865 (April 18–24, 1962).

Diatkine, Anne, and Gérard Lefort. "Varda, la glaneuse vagabonde." *Libération*, May 15, 2002.

Domenach, Elise, and Philippe Rouyer. "Entretien avec Agnès Varda: Passer sous le pont des Arts à la voile." *Positif* 574 (December 2008): 17–21.

Egly, Max. "Comment Présenter le film, conduire la discussion dans un ciné-club." In *Regards neufs sur le cinéma*, edited by Jacques Chevalier and Max Egly, 253–63. Paris: Seuil, Peuple et Culture, 1963.

European Audiovisual Observatory. *Focus 2008 World Film Market Trends*. Strasbourg: Council of Europe, 2008.

Fabry, Julie. Interview with author. June 2012, Paris.

"La FFCC à la rue." *Cinéma 62* 66 (May 1962): 149–52.

Fiant, Antony, Roxane Hamery and Eric Thounvenel, eds. *Agnès Varda: Le cinéma et au-delà*. Rennes: Presses Universitaires de Rennes, 2009.

Flitterman-Lewis, Sandy. *To Desire Differently: Feminism and the French Cinema*. Expanded Edition. New York: Columbia University Press, 1996.

Frodon, Jean-Michel. "La caméra numérique force les cinéastes à ouvrir l'oeil." *Le Monde*, August 15, 2001.

———. "Cinémamusée: Le grand tournant," *Cahiers du cinéma* 611 (April 2006): 8.

Gorbman, Claudia. "Finding a Voice: Varda's Early Travelogues." *SubStance* 41:2 (2012): 40–57.

———. "Varda's Music." *Music and the Moving Image* 1.3 (Fall 2008): 27–34.

Graumier, Vincent. "Les Mouvements de Ciné-clubs en France, 1945–1968." Mémoire de D.E.A., Université de Paris X, Nanterre, 1993.

Gross, Laura. "Losing at Scrabble, Winning at French." In *Francophonia: Stories from the Professional French Masters Program*, 43–58, edited by Ritt Deitz. Madison, Wisc.: Incidence Editions, 2014.

Hayward, Susan. "Beyond the Gaze and into Femme-Filmécriture: Agnès Varda's *Sans toit ni loi*." In *French Film: Texts and Contexts*, 269–80. Edited by Susan Hayward and Ginette Vincendeau. London: Routledge, 1990.

Jacobs, Steven. *Framing Pictures: Film and the Visual Arts*. Edinburgh: University of Edinburgh Press, 2012.

Jeander. [No title]. In Denis Marison, *Le Cinéma par ceux qui le font*. Paris: Librairie Arthème Fayard, 1949.

Jürgensen, Jacob Dahl. "50th Venice Biennale." *Frieze* 77 (September 2003). http://www.frieze.com/issue/review/jacob_dahl_juergensen/. Accessed June 1, 2015.

Kaganski, Serge. "Les Glaneurs et la glaneuse, le ciné-brocante d'Agnès Varda." *Les Inrockuptibles* (July 4, 2000): 28–32.

Kast, Pierre. "Répandre le goût du cinéma, faire connaître ses chefs d'oeuvre, éduquer le public: telle est la tâche des ciné-clubs," *L'Ecran français* 18 (Oct. 31, 1945): 15; cited in Vincent Graumier, "Les Mouvements de Ciné-clubs en France, 1945–1968," Mémoire de D.E.A. Université de Paris X, Nanterre, 1993, 46.

Kelly, Brendan. "The Gleaners and I." *Variety* 379:2 (May 19, 2000): 26.

King, Homay. "Matter, Time, and the Digital: Varda's *The Gleaners and I*." *Quarterly Review of Film and Video* 24.5 (Fall 2007): 421–429.

Kleiner, Fred S. *Gardner's Art Through the Ages: A Concise Western History*, 3rd ed. Boston: Wadsworth/Cengage Learning, 2013.

Kline, T. Jefferson. *Agnès Varda: Interviews*. Jackson: University Press of Mississippi, 2014.

Ledoux, Jacques. Transcription. Interview with Agnès Varda. Cinémathèque Royale de Belgique / Radio-Télévision-Belge, 1961–62. Ciné-Tamaris Archive.

Loyer, Emmanuelle. *Le théâtre citoyen de Jean Vilar: une utopie d'après-guerre*. Paris: Presses Universitaires de France, 1997.

Marcabru, Pierre. "Cannes: Festival des valeurs sûres: Un seul film vraiment original, Cléo de 5 à 7." *Arts* 869 (May 16–22, 1962).

Marcia, Claude. "Soi et l'autre (*Les Glaners et La Glaneuse*), *Agnès Varda: le cinéma et au-delà*." Edited by Antony Fiant, Roxanne Hamery, and Eric Thouvenel, 43–48. Rennes: Presses Universitaires de Rennes, 2009.

Mardiguian, Georges. "*La Pointe courte*: Mes premières armes dans la prise de son." *L'Ecole central de T.S.F. et d'électronique* 29 (April 1955).

McNeill, Isabelle. *Memory and the Moving Image: French Film in the Digital Era.* Edinburgh: Edinburgh University Press, 2010.

Michael, Charlie. *French Blockbusters: Globalization, National Cinema and the Discourses of "Cultural Diversity."* Dissertation. University of Wisconsin–Madison, 2010.

Millard, Kathryn. "After the Typewriter: The Screenplay in a Digital Era." *Journal of Screenwriting* 1:1 (September 2009): 11–25.

———. *Screenwriting in a Digital Era.* London: Palgrave MacMillan, 2014.

Neupert, Richard. *A History of the French New Wave Cinema.* 2nd ed. Madison: University of Wisconsin Press, 2007.

Nichols, Bill. *Representing Reality.* Bloomington: Indiana University Press, 1992.

Orpen, Valerie. *Cléo de 5 à 7.* Urbana: University of Illinois Press, 2007.

Païni, Dominique. "Du montage exposé: Le Triptique de Noirmoutier, 2005." In Agnès Varda, *L'île et elle, Regards sur l'exposition*, 34. Arles: Actes Sud, 2006.

"Peuple et Culture." In *Regards neufs sur le cinéma*, edited by Jacques Chevalier and Max Egly, 314–16. Paris: Seuil, Peuple et Culture, 1963.

Philipe, Claude-Jean, and Evelyne Pagès. Interview with Agnès Varda, Sandrine Bonnaire, and Macha Méril. R.T.L. Emission "Cinéma," December 7, 1985.

Piazzo, Philippe. "Agnès varda, glaneuse sachant glaner." *Aden/Le Monde*, July 5–11, 2000.

Pinel, Vincent. *Introduction au Ciné-club: histoire, théorie, pratique du Ciné-club en France.* Paris: Editions Ouvrières, 1964.

Porcile, François. "Commandes avouées, commandes masquées: la production française de courts métrages de de Gaulle à de Gaulle." In *Le court métrage documentaire français de 1945 à 1968, Créations et créateurs*, edited by Dominique Bluher and Philippe Pilard, 13–23. Rennes: Presses universitaires de Rennes / Agence du court métrage, 2009.

Prédal, René. *Sans toit ni loi d'Agnès Varda.* Clefs concours—Cinéma. Paris: Atlande, 2003.

Regards neufs sur le cinéma. Edited by Jacques Chevalier and Max Egly. Paris: Peuple et culture, Seuil, 1963.

Régnier, Philippe. "Agnès Varda, la 'dame patate'," La cinéaste présente une installation à Venise." *Journal des arts*, June 27, 2003.

Rose, Cecilia, production director for *Les Plages d'Agnès.* Interview with author, Paris, December 8, 2009.

Rosello, Mireille. "Agnès Varda's *Les Glaneurs et la glaneuse.*" *Studies in French Cinema* 1.1 (2001): 30.

Royer, Philippe. "Agnès Varda a retrouvé ses glaneurs." *La Croix*, December 17, 2002.

Servat, Henry-Jean. "Errance sur les routes du Sud." *Midi Libre*, December 2, 1985.

Simsi, Simon. *Ciné-Passions.* Paris: Editions Dixit, 2012.

Smith, Alison. *Agnès Varda.* Manchester: Manchester University Press, 1998.

Tailleur, Roger. "*Cleo*: From Here to Eternity." In *Positif, 50 Years: Selections from the French Film Journal*, edited by Michel Ciment and Laurence Kardish, 73–82. New York: Museum of Modern Art, 2002.

Thouvenal, Eric. "L'Opéra-Mouffe: le ventre de Paris, ou la cinemïeutique d'Agnès Varda." In *Le court métrage documentaire français de 1945 à 1968, Créations et créateurs*, edited by Dominique Bluher and Philippe Pilard, 183–93. Rennes: Presses universitaires de Rennes / Agence du court métrage, 2009.

Trémois, Claude-Marie. "Les Glaneurs et la glaneuse d'Agnès Varda." *Esprit* (July 2000): 185–87.

Truffaut, François. "La Pointe Courte d'Agnès Varda." *Arts*, January 1956.

Ungar, Steven. *Cléo de 5 à 7*. London: Palgrave MacMillan and BFI, 2008.

Utopia Station, Press Kit, La Biennale di Venezia, 50th International Art Exhibition, 15th June–2nd November 2003. http://universes-in-universe.de/car/venezia/bien50/utopia/e-press.htm. Accessed June 1, 2015.

"Varda à Saisir." *Il était 2 fois*, no. 5, June 17, 1985.

Varda, Agnès. *Agnès Varda: L'île et elle*. Exhibition catalogue. Fondation Cartier pour l'art contemporain. Arles: Editions Acte Sud, 2006.

———. Ciné-Tamaris Archive, *Cléo de 5 à 7*.

———. Ciné-Tamaris Archive, *Du côté de la côte*.

———. Ciné-Tamaris Archive, *Les Glaneurs et la glaneuse*.

———. Ciné-Tamaris Archive, *L'île et elle*.

———. Ciné-Tamaris Archive, *L'Opéra-Mouffe*.

———. Ciné-Tamaris Archive, *Ô saisons, Ô chateaux*.

———. Ciné-Tamaris Archive, *Patatutopia*.

———. Ciné-Tamaris Archive, *Les Plages d'Agnès*.

———. Ciné-Tamaris Archive, *La Pointe Courte*.

———. Ciné-Tamaris Archive, *Sans toit ni loi*.

———. *La Côte d'Azur*. Paris: Les Editions du Temps, 1961.

———. "Director's Note." Zeitgeist Press Kit, 2000.

———. "Filming *The Gleaners*." Zeitgeist Press Kit, 2000.

———. "Hommage à André Bazin." Festival de Cannes 1983. *Les Cahiers du cinéma* (April 1983).

———. *L'île et elle*, proposal. Ciné-Tamaris Archive.

———. *L'île et elle, Regards sur l'exposition*. Fondation Cartier pour l'art contemporain. Arles: Actes Sud, 2006.

———. "La moissonneuse-battante." *Les Inrockuptibles* 270 (December 19–25, 2000): 73.

———. Personal interview with the author, July 2003.

———. Personal interview with the author, June 2013.

———. "*Les Plages d'Agnès* (ou Aventures d'un Autoportrait)." Scénario Original. July 16, 2007. Ciné-Tamaris Archive.

———. Les plages d'Agnès, promotional pamphlet, Ciné-Tamaris. 2008.

———. "Présenté par Agnès," Introduction to *L'Opéra-Mouffe*, DVD, Varda Tous Courts.

———. Video interview. *La Pointe Courte*. DVD. *4 by Agnès Varda* boxed set, the Criterion Collection, 2007.

———. *Varda par Agnès*. Paris: Editions Cahiers du cinéma and Ciné-Tamaris, 1994.

Varda, Agnès, and Sandrine Bonnaire. "Un lion d'or pour *Sans toit ni loi*, Radio interview, Oroleis Paris / EVB—FR3." December 1985.

Veinstein, Alain. Radio interview with Agnès Varda, Nathalie Sarraute, Macha Méril, Jacques Demy. "La Nuit sur un plateau." *France-Culture*, January 7, 1986.

Vesey, Alyx. "Waste Not: Les Glaneurs et la Glaneuse and the Heterogenous Documentary Film Score." *Studies in French Cinema* 14.3 (2014): 167–79 .

Wilson, Emma. *Alain Resnais*. Manchester: Manchester University Press, 2006.

Index

Kelley Conway is a professor of communication arts at the University of Wisconsin–Madison. She is the author of *Chanteuse in the City: The Realist Singer in French Film.*

Books in the series Contemporary Film Directors

The University of Illinois Press
is a founding member of the
Association of American University Presses.

_____

Composed in 10/13 New Caledonia
with Helvetica Neue display
by Lisa Connery
at the University of Illinois Press
Manufactured by Cushing-Malloy, Inc.

University of Illinois Press
1325 South Oak Street
Champaign, IL 61820-6903
www.press.uillinois.edu